BITTERSWEET

Also by Luise Eichenbaum and Susie Orbach
UNDERSTANDING WOMEN   *Penguin*
WHAT DO WOMEN WANT?   *Fontana*

and by Susie Orbach
FAT IS A FEMINIST ISSUE   *Arrow*
FAT IS A FEMINIST ISSUE II   *Arrow*
HUNGER STRIKE   *Faber and Faber*

BITTERSWEET

*Facing up to feelings of love, envy
and competition in women's friendships*

Susie Orbach and Luise Eichenbaum

CENTURY
LONDON MELBOURNE AUCKLAND JOHANNESBURG

First published in 1987 by Century Hutchinson Ltd
62 – 65 Chandos Place
London WC2N 4NW

Century Hutchinson Australia Pty Ltd,
PO Box 496, 16 – 22 Church Street, Hawthorn, Victoria 3122,
Australia

Century Hutchinson New Zealand Limited,
PO Box 40 – 086, Glenfield, Auckland 10, New Zealand

Century Hutchinson South Africa (Pty) Ltd,
PO Box 337, Bergvlei, 2012 South Africa

Typeset by Inforum Ltd, Portsmouth
Printed and bound in Great Britain by Anchor Brendon Ltd,
Tiptree, Essex

British Library Cataloguing in Publication Data
Orbach, Susie
Bittersweet : facing up to feelings of love,
envy and competition in women's friendships.
1. Women   2. Interpersonal relations
I. Title   II. Eichenbaum, Luise
305.4'2   HQ1233

ISBN 0–7126–1476–1

DEDICATION

This book is written in recognition of our relationship, our deep love for one another and in the hope that it will speak to other women.

ACKNOWLEDGEMENTS

The authors would like to thank Gillian Slovo, Joseph Schwartz and Caradoc King for their enthusiasm and labour at the beginning of the project, and Jeremy Pikser for his constructive comments, time, and energy in the last push.

Contents

Author's Note

This book is an attempt to provide a feminist psycho-analytic understanding of the emotional and psychological processes that are set in train when women perceive differences in each other. It is about the difficulties women face in coming to terms with those differences.

It is *not* an account of differences between women. We have not attempted to discuss the particulars of class, race and sexual orientation as they create divisions between women. Differences in background and in present status between women are of course substantial and contribute to the hurt, the misunderstandings and the anger that fester in women's relationships today. The assumptions we make about one another often do not take account of each other's or our own particular circumstances. The expectations, desires and ambitions we have for ourselves are based on a perception of the world seen from the vantage point of an individual's class background, her economic situation, her sexual orientation, her race, the ambience of her family of origin, her age, her physical abilities and her physical disabilities. We are often blind and ignorant *vis-à-vis* experiences disimilar to our own, we may deny differences, we may misperceive the circumstances of others or we may collude with stereotypes in our ignorance. Certainly lesbians, working-class women, black women and disabled women have suffered by being described thoughtlessly and stereotypically. Certainly lesbians, working-class women, black women and disabled women are often unwittingly written out of the accounts of women's psychology in general because of a failure to include them either by reference to the commonality of women's experience or by reference to the particular of their experiences.

Our intention in writing this book has been to enable women to handle those differences more productively and less destructively than is often the case at present. We hope that we are writing for all women, but we well understand that our conclusions reflect the scope and the limits of our clinical work in the UK and the USA. We write about the women we have met in the course of our work; women who come from a wide range of backgrounds, differing political persuasions and sexual orientations. We have worked with women mainly white, but some black, a few asian, between the ages of twenty and sixty. Some have had no formal education past the age of sixteen, others are first generation educated working-class, many were newly professional women, many are or have been housewives, some are 'unemployed', and still others were women involved in their own or their husband's businesses. Family circumstances have varied just as widely. Some women, heterosexual and lesbian, are living on their own, some are living with their children, some are living with their own and/or their male or female partners children, some are divorced. We have encountered these women in long-term psychotherapy, in short-term therapy, in couple therapy, in workshop settings, in conferences and in work-based consultations.

We very much hope that women of all backgrounds, sexual orientations and ages will find points of identity with the women we are writing about even if their own particular circumstances are not adequately described. We hope women will be able to read this as an *inclusive* account, and take what may be useful in our analysis into their own situation where specific differences in social and personal categories can be explored in more detail.

Susie Orbach and Luise Eichenbaum, April 1987

Introduction

With three-quarters of the book done, we need to begin again. We need to make a new beginning because too many things are stuck. The ideas, the theory, is all there. We know it inside out. We are still in the ideas together even though we no longer share them on a daily basis. That was always one of the pleasures. Our minds were so in synch. One would have an idea and start the sentence, the other could finish it. We thought that writing a book on women's friendships this year – the year in which we had to face our living in different places – would be the way to insure our link, the involved attachment. We wanted a project which we could share, which would enable us to keep our working partnership alive, which represented what we understood about difficulties women today were facing. But somewhere in that decision was also the denial of the reality that we do not share our daily lives. We do not share the lives of our children. We do not share in the daily lives of our work. Where once we knew what filled the other's days and concerns. Now we cannot. For now an ocean is between us.

This book is about the lives of women and their relationships with one another in the 1980s. It is about the legacy we carry from generations of women before us as emotional caregivers, daughters, mothers, domestic labourers. It is about the rich ways in which women give to each other. It is about the ways in which women connect easily and intimately. It is about the pleasures and fun women share together. It is about the virtues of femininity. It is, at the same time, about the lives of contemporary White, Black, Asian and Latin women in

1

the Western world whose social roles have been dramatically changing in the last eighteen years. It is about the meeting ground of those two worlds and the psychological reactions, conflicts, and struggles in which women today inevitably find themselves. It is, above all, about the ways in which these transformations on the social and psychological levels are affecting women's relationships with one another.

When we met fifteen years ago, when Luise was nineteen and Susie twenty-five, we created the air of being 'free women'. We were full of the headiness of the early days of feminism and we involved ourselves in projects that women would benefit from. We spent much of our days with other women learning and developing the new field of women's studies, discovering together a new way to see our personal histories and challenging our automatic responses to almost everything. With an air that felt risky and electrifying, we gave priority to our female friendships.

The world of the early 1970s in which we met turned our lives and our views of most things upside down. As a generation we put into practice things that had been outside our imagination just a few years before. As students, our time was flexible. We spent whole days and nights with our friends, secure in the knowledge that our love affairs with men would co-exist with our important female friendships, and that if they didn't (the ones with men, that is), it was the men who would have to adjust and change in dramatic ways.

We remember the first times we saw each other at Richmond College[1] of the City University of New York. Susie was in a seminar. A young woman undergraduate read a paragraph she had prepared for an upcoming event to celebrate International Women's Day 1971. It was a powerful and passionate statement. Susie turned to her friend Carol Bloom, the Women's Studies coordinator. "Wow, that was good." She asked, "Who's she?" "Oh that's Luise Eichenbaum, she's in Women's Studies too."

2

And then, at a class on women in film, a young woman with a long suede skirt, high purple boots, trendy London layered haircut, an English accent, confidently commented on the film and what it had to say about women's lives, which stirred Luise. "Who *is* she?" Luise asked Carol. "That's Susie Orbach", replied Carol. "She's English and into politics and law and psychology." Luise was interested.

A friendship was about to begin that would affect us in profound ways for the next decade and a half of our lives. That special bond that formed in the earliest years of our friendship and the intensity of feeling between us continues still. The desire to chatter and share, to fill each other in on everything and seek each other's views vibrates between us. Like women all over the world we practice that particularly 'feminine' skill of holding ten conversations and activities in our heads at the same time.

Our common work at the beginning of our friendship involved helping to build the Women's Studies Programme. With our dearest friend Carol Bloom and the other women in the department we were engaged in creating the first Bachelor of Arts degree in this new field. It was an energetic department which, for a brief time, was expressive of the very best energy of the Student and Women's Liberation Movements. Students became teachers, social barriers lessened and women began to study and learn together in circumstances of their own making. It was an exciting time. New educational policy was in the making and we were the makers.

But the Programme itself was headed for unanticipated difficulties. It had come into existence despite strong opposition from the college administration. The reality of a successful programme soon gave way to internal dissension and strife. The unity between the women, which had been such an essential feature of the success in setting up the Programme, was soon shown to be ephemeral. It was a unity against the administration, rather than the expression of well thought out common

3

educational ideas. Political differences then took on tremendous significance and caucuses soon formed. Three factions disputed the running of the programme, crippling it. Meetings reeked of betrayal and anger. The women, all unused to wielding power within institutional settings, seemed set upon destroying their common project.

We were shocked, devastated and shaken up. How could women, apparently with so much in common, be so destructive? How had our unity turned into a battlefield so very fast? What was the origin of the rage and disappointment that this dispute unleashed?

Perplexed and concerned, we were motivated to learn more about how psychological elements could be at play between women. Women's rational and conscious lives had become far more comprehensible the more we understood about our social position. Yet we remained in the dark over the deeper workings of women's unconscious lives and the ways in which they were entwined with those of other women. Our friendship and participation in the factional disputes of the Programme brought us closer together and strengthened our commitment to understanding both how the 'outside got inside and the inside got outside' [2].

For the next few years we were immersed in a new project – the study of women's psychology. And within this general project we had a particular interest in understanding the tension between women's strong and loving feelings for one another and the enmity that could suddenly occur. Together with other women who were feminists and psychotherapists[3], we studied Freud and his theories of psychoanalysis (although they were generally unpopular amongst feminists at the time); we studied humanistic psychology and alternative therapies which were popular at the time; we went on to postgraduate studies and brought our interests about feminism and women's psychology into the classrooms. Throughout each area of study a feminist perspective lead us to analyse, re-evaluate and re-interpret the

4

theories of psychological development. With a perspective that understood women's social position, we began to develop a practice of psychotherapy, that could address the intricacies of women's complicated inner and outer lives.

When, several years later in 1976, we opened the Women's Therapy Centre in London, our intention was to provide psychotherapy which more appropriately addressed the needs of women. Concerned lest we wouldn't attract clients, we made up flyers, sent out press releases, spoke on radio about why we saw the need for this kind of psychotherapeutic service. We were stunned by the response. The Centre attracted all sorts of women from different age groups and class backgrounds[4]. Some came who had previously been in psychotherapy but felt they had either had bad experiences or ones which were just not terribly helpful. It attracted women who strongly identified as feminists and who now felt they could begin psychotherapy with a degree of trust and safety. Women came and sought therapy who had no involvement in feminism but who responded because they read an interview, or heard us speak, about an aspect of their lives with which they could strongly identify. But, even with the initial response to the service, we had no idea of the enormity of the success the Centre would achieve. (It is now in its 11th year, receives both public and private funding and is staffed by nearly a dozen psychotherapists and several administrators.)

And our relationship grew. We were now united in a joint project which was stimulating, engaging, time consuming. The popularity of the Centre found us involving two new psychotherapists, Sally Berry and Margaret Green, within just a few months of our opening. Later that year we took on two more, Margot Waddell who was finishing her training at the Tavistock Clinic and the late Pam Smith who came to us on secondment from the North London Polytechnic. Sheila Ernst was soon to join us as a trainee. We organised seminars for professionals on the psychology of women and workshops for the

5

public. We were thriving. Until the following spring.

It seemed to begin out of the blue. We started feeling irritated with one another. Luise didn't like the way Susie could be curt on the phone. Susie didn't like the way Luise hesitated over things. We began to look at one another critically, as lovers often do when the honeymoon is over. We began to snap at one another. The negative vibes increased daily. Each night we went home to our men and complained to them about the outrageous habits of the other. Partners, best friends. What was happening?

As it had in the Women's Studies Programme at Richmond, the success of the project seemed to engender new, surprising problems. We spent three months of agony in the same small office but not knowing how to talk to one another. We did not know how to confront each other directly with the truth of our feelings. It was a torturous time. Finally there was some reprieve – summer vacation was approaching and Luise decided to go back to the States for a visit.

In that month apart we complained about each other to friends, each frightened and unsure of what the outcome was going to be. But the distance also allowed for other feelings to emerge. Missing. Loneliness. Pain. Hurt. Longing. When Luise walked through the door on a September morning, we looked at each other, paused, searched for a shared warm response. Then came the hug and the tears. Lots of tears. We declared our love, how we had missed each other; not only during the month, but throughout the four or five months. And then we talked. And then we yelled.

In the final analysis we saw that there was a common denominator to our anger. We each felt that the other was continually making assumptions. Luise thought that Susie assumed her agreement about things, without asking her or checking to see if she was in agreement or not. She seemed not to be aware sometimes that Luise had her own opinions. Susie felt that Luise assumed that Susie would take care of her in certain ways, taking the

6

caregiving for granted, as if Susie were her invisible magic mother, doing things for her without needing to be appreciated. We each felt lost inside the relationship. Not seen. We were no longer *individuated*. In some powerful way our lives had been joined and even *merged*. We had not managed to stay separate while birthing our new 'baby', The Women's Therapy Centre. Our withdrawal and anger over a period of months was our attempt to separate ourselves, to distinguish us, one from the other. And yet if we had only retreated – as we were tempted to do – that would have meant the end of our relationship. Scared and anxious, we forced ourselves to struggle, to confront, to speak up directly to the other. We were lucky. Somewhere we were still aware of our need and love for another. We knew we had to say don't make assumptions, I am not you, I am not your mother, I am a separate person. We wondered why saying such things to one another was so very difficult. We did not know then what a critical lesson we had learned by bridging that chasm in our relationship.

Now it's 1987, ten years after that first fight. There have been a few more when we've each felt disregarded, misunderstood or taken for granted. They are less frightening now and they build up over days rather than months. But they are still difficult to handle in the midst of the love and commitment we have towards one another. By now we've been best friends for over fifteen years.

We've each lived and worked together in one another's countries. In 1981, with our old friend Carol Bloom, we started up The Women's Therapy Centre Institute in New York to train psychotherapists[5]. But while the two Centres are a visible expression of the work we have done and do together, today we live an ocean apart. The three thousand miles between London and New York mean the loss of daily relating, of leisurely talking on the phone as many times as need be, of seeing each other at work, of preparing suppers together, of taking the kids to the zoo together, of travelling around either continent giving talks together, of shopping and chatting. There is pleasure at being able to present our work to a new audience; pain that we are doing so alone. Each paper written in a joint name evokes the pain of the separation. Each time Lukas (Susie's son) calls for Gina (Luise's daughter) or Gina for Lukas, tears are shed on one or other side of the Atlantic. The children are only little, but have already absorbed the importance of their mother's friendship.

Writing this book on women's relationships – the hope, the promise, the love, the grief, the anguish and the disappointments – the reparative nature of them and the damaging aspects of them – had to start with a brief account of our relationship. For we write this book partly in celebration of the relationship we have enjoyed with each other and with our other women friends, the pleasures that have come from working in female-centred environments and the wish to acknowledge the achievements of women at this particular moment in Western history.

Contemporary women's friendships have been forged at a time when women's role has been changing and women are demanding of themselves that they get out and fulfill themselves. It wasn't until the seventies that the significance of women's relationships were recognised and given priority. Of course women's friendships have always been important and essential in their lives but, until the seventies, friendship between women was rarely graced with the social recognition that befitted it. Friendships were fitted around family commitments, and almost every woman understood that her time with a friend was framed in this way.

While this new acceptance of the importance of women's relationships may not have been conscious in everyone's mind, so that many women continued to be isolated in this period as they had been before, it is nevertheless the general case that women's relationships are now acknowledged as terribly important. American films made in the 70s such as *Girlfriends, Alice Doesn't Live*

8

Here Anymore, the French film *One Sings, the Other Doesn't*, the Norwegian film *Wives* and the television projects hatched at that time which came to our screens in recent years (*Rhoda, Kate & Allie, Mary Tyler Moore* come to mind), reflect on a cultural level this shift in significance of the role and place of women's friendships. In these films, women friends were shown confiding in one another, laughing with one another and commiserating with one another. The friendships are not portrayed as a stopgap between sexual relationships but as a significant part of a woman's life. Indeed for many women, woman to woman relationships have become primary. Many women, who a few years ago would have found it impossible to act on sexual feelings they might have had towards one another, now allow the erotic side of their feelings to emerge. Today, even though there is still considerable discrimination, lesbian relationships are becoming more visible and commonplace. For many women, closeness with a woman and the intimacy she finds in her friendship is deeply sustaining.

But paradoxically, while the media has presented female friendships with some accuracy, those very friendships are facing new difficulties that make them less ideal, less easy, than they were a decade ago. Where a decade ago, there was something deeply liberatory about sharing our difficulties with one another, supporting one another in moving forward and struggling, challenging each other and so on. Today an ocean of misunderstanding can exist between women.

Part of our project has been to unravel and uncover the difficulties between women today, to address the sticky issues in women's relationships, the messy uncomfortable bits one wishes would just disappear. We need to face the hurt, the envy, the competition, the unexpressed anger, the feelings of betrayal and the experience of abandonment. For, along with the recognition of the importance of women's relationships in the last decade and a half, has been the discovery that these relationships are not as easy and troublefree as we would wish.

Behind the curtain of sisterhood lies a myriad of emotional tangles which are presently causing havoc in women's relationships with each other. The hope we have invested in our relationships with one another, and the searing upset we suffer when they disappoint us, must be understood in a context that respects and honours these relationships.

Connectedness, attachment, affiliation, selflessness, have been and still are, to a great extent, the foundations of women's experience. A woman knows herself and gathers a sense of well-being through her connection and attachment to others. For the past decade and a half or so, women *en masse* have been struggling to become more autonomous, more independent. Enormous amounts of time and energy have been and are currently being devoted to careers, education, advancement in areas which had previously been the domain of men. Although the social environment is one which appears more accepting of women's autonomy, the external prohibitions run deep. Women themselves embody these restrictions and constraints. And, as women try to free themselves from the internal and external restraints, they find themselves acutely aware of the successes and achievements of other women. Women gauge and measure themselves in relation to friends, workmates, neighbours. Does she manage a job, a relationship and children? How? My best friend has a child, will I be able to? How much money does she earn? How does she manage to keep herself looking so well and fit when I feel exhausted? She seems so confident and self-assured while I feel like a fraud, a kid dressed up in grown-ups clothes. These are the kinds of questions that are haunting women on a daily basis. All too painfully many women feel keenly aware of the emergence of feelings of competition, of envy, of anger, of abandonment in relation to their women friends. Feelings which serve to distance women, not bring them together. Feelings which feel too ugly, too unacceptable to talk about.

To suddenly feel a paralysing guilt towards a friend

10

whose life seems to be going badly; to fear attack from those on whose support you rely, to notice envious feelings exploding inside oneself; to be experienced as a betrayer; to feel competitive with one's closest friend; to experience terror that other women will abandon you or chop you down; feelings such as these are becoming commonplace. The feelings of guilt, of competition, of anger, of envy, of betrayal, and of jealosy that women are capable of stirring up in each other are formidable. They are intensely experienced, and if they are not worked through, they are inevitably damaging. They erode and poison companionship. They threaten to destroy the openness and trust that can exist between women.

Women are making the shift from being people who service others, defer to others and who know themselves through their attachment to others, to becoming people who are visible in their own right and who stand as separate individuals while still connected to others. This is no easy feat. It is, however, what hundreds of thousands of women are engaged in doing either self-consciously or because of the impact of social forces on their lives. In this important struggle for change, we must not repudiate those who have most helped us get where we are today – women. But neither should we be squeamish about confronting the very real difficulties that can occur between women. Without sentimentalizing women's relationships, we can still declare women's continuing need of one another. Women need each other's support and permission for the autonomy and self-development they are pursuing. They need each other to talk through the difficulties they are experiencing on so many fronts. They need to explore the now hidden feelings between women which are contaminating women's relationships. We can and must take on these issues. In so doing we can preserve and nurture that which is a most important relationship to us – woman to woman.

References

1. Now incorporated into the College of Staten Island, The City University of New York.
2. See Luise Eichenbaum & Susie Orbach, *Understanding Women: A feminist Psychoanalytic Approach* (Penguin, 1982), formerly called, *Inside Out Outside In*.
3. The New York Feminist Therapists Study Group (1973–75).
4. The Centre has not attracted many Black or Asian women. This is most likely because there have been no Black therapists on the staff who might provide an easier bridge for Black women seeking therapy.
5. Over the last five years we've been joined by Susan Gutwill, Anne Leiner, Andrea Gitter and Lela Zaphiropoulos.

CHAPTER 1

Bittersweet

"Happy endings begin here," insisted Julie, a thirty-five year old drama teacher, towards the end of a Women's Therapy Centre workshop on difficulties in women's friendships. "They begin here, in the confrontation of our negative feelings towards women we care about, not in fairy tale endings which suppress disagreement and pretend that everything is alright."

Although the Centre has a wide range of workshop topics covering numerous aspects of women's lives to-day, enrolling in a workshop on difficulties in women's friendships undoubtedly engenders feelings of anxiety and fear for the participants. Thirteen women gathered together to talk about the pain of jealousy, the pain of envy, the pain of anger, the pain of competition, the pain of abandonment, the pain of betrayal and the pain of wanting, when felt in relation to women. The upset in the room was palpable. Women were daring to face their negative feelings towards each other.

There were feelings of shame and disloyalty: "How can I be discussing my best friend with a group of strangers?" There was hesitation: "I don't know if I can put words to this feeling . . . I hate feeling this way but I really am so hurt . . .," there were feelings of bitterness and rage: "I am furious, how could she do that to me . . .?" There were feelings of being exploited: "How could she expect me to give and give and then not be there for me when I need her?" There were feelings of disappointment, of not being seen, of not being allowed to change, of sudden disapproval, of unaccountable and unexpected hurt. The workshop participants were emotionally bruised. But as they engaged in the process of trying to understand what went wrong, whether friendship would always turn out this way, there was a relief, stemming from the honest realization that women *do* have conflicting feelings for each other. The workshop was timely. A decade of open recognition of the importance and nurturing quality of women's friendships made it just safe enough to explore the underbelly of these relationships.

Julie described her amazement at seeing such a workshop on the Women's Therapy Centre schedule. It allowed shameful and impermissible feelings to be aired. But, she worried, would the whole world know she had negative feelings towards her dear friend if she enrolled for the workshop? Might she bump into someone on the way there, or worse still, at the workshop itself, thus exposing her conflicting feelings? Others shared her apprehension but reasoned that, if the workshop was listed, it must mean *other* women felt the same way. *Other* women were in pain, angry, disappointed. Public recognition of these difficult feelings brought a great sense of relief.

Eleanor, a journalist in her thirties, wept as she talked of the fury she felt towards her friend Anne, who had recently taken up with a new man. Everything she thought their friendship stood for was now swept aside, as Anne broke dates and filled up their telephone conversations with gushing bulletins about the previous night's tryst. Really, it was too much, this going on about Jack. Christ, he wasn't even that interesting! "I know I might be jealous," said Eleanor, "but that's not the whole story. He's such a jerk. He isn't anywhere near good enough for her but here she is head over heels and jettisoning our friendship or, at least, relegating it to the back burner. It feels like such a betrayal. It's not that I

14

don't understand her infatuation and involvement or wish her well with it, I honestly do. It's just that I feel so pushed aside, not discarded exactly, but like all of a sudden my function has changed. I'm there for her to replay it, so she can savour the sex and the excitement all over again as she tells me. Even that I could understand but I don't like not doing things together anymore. We don't go to the movies or plays, she and Jack do. We don't go out to a new restaurant, she and Jack do. I know I sound petty but I do feel our friendship didn't mean to her what it meant to me, if she could just put it aside when he came along. It's like she was just using it as a stopgap, not a pleasure in itself. I thought that was precisely what we weren't going to do".

"I feel let down and pushed out too," said another woman, "but I tend to see it as more my fault. Perhaps I was expecting too much from my friend Ruth. I have the feeling that I become so involved with my close friends that I almost push them away through the intensity of need I bring to the relationship. Ruth and I used to see each other every day, we were in and out of each other's houses, borrowing children, milk, cars, lawn mowers and sharing emotional traumas with each other. After we'd talked about it for months, Ruth went back to College and she really turned her back on me. At first I thought she was so caught up in the newness of what she was doing and the work she had to face, that I understood and tried to give her a bit of space. But when I had a crisis in my life; my mother was dying and I was very broken up about it. I told Ruth – well she could see I wasn't coping too well – and she was kind but cold. Instead of rallying around she sort of told me to pull myself together. I was shocked and hurt. I felt so rejected. I felt like a big fat ugly mass of need but I wasn't sure who was right or wrong. I'm still not and that's why I'm here. I thought she would stand by me. Perhaps that's the nub of the problem. I have such high expectations of my friendships with women. I expect them to be giving and flexible. I felt I could understand her need for

15

some distance when she started College, but why couldn't she help me when my mother was dying? These high hopes I have of women really confuse me. That's why I still feel so tortured after a year."

The internal dialogue, thought about so many times as a way to understand the pain, to soothe the hurt, is voiced out loud now in this workshop setting with thirteen other women. There is something soothing in itself about having other women eager to listen.

What happened in each of these friendships? How did they turn from supportive, nurturing mainstays to bitter disappointments? What is it that makes women's friendships what they are – both bitter and sweet?

Let's begin at the beginning. Two women meet, perhaps at a party, a class, over a garden fence, or at a new job. They share a mutual interest and, with characteristic feminine social agility, they extend their initial point of interest to other matters. Their conversation takes account of the emotional climate of the subject matter. Thoughts and feelings about work, children, husbands, boyfriends, lovers, mothers, entertaining, cooking, politics, sex, music, about aspirations, sport, fashion, suffuse their conversation. Their emotions are intrinsic to the contact. They make up a patoiṣ – a distinctively women's language. Confidences are readily and easily shared, assumptions made about difficult emotional states, disappointments acknowledged and solutions sought. Women unguardedly confide in each other with an ease that often astounds men. Sharing is not a concession, a particularly difficult struggle, an extraction; rather it is part and parcel of women's relating. It is second nature, a habit, a way of being. Not sharing feels odd, a holding back that feels almost like a betrayal.

The texture of women's relationships, from the most intimate friendships and love relationships to the most cursory of acquaintances contain within them the similar elements of compassion, sympathy, and identification. It is these elements, the emotional gullies in which much

16

of female living occurs, that allows us to talk of a specifically female culture that has the capacity to embrace all women. Women can share intimacies with each other without much hesitation or embarrassment. From adolescence onwards young women have tried to understand, with one another, the world around them. Female friendships have taken on enormous significance and prominence.

Decisions and desires are discussed extensively. Young women digest the adult world they are poised to enter together. They seek a bosom pal with whom they can giggle about the new identities they are inventing and practising. Closeness with a peer becomes imperative. As they seek their place in the world they do so much as generations of young women before them. They conceive of it within a network of relationships. They take on school, dating, college, marriage, a first job, with the enabling hand of a female friend. Perhaps a temporary friend soon to be forgotten, but whatever its longevity or circumstances, female companionship has, more than likely, been a distinctive feature of most women's lives.

In their journey through life, women look for and find female companionship. Within their friendships they talk uninhibitedly with each other about the details of sex, about what they want and what they have in their love relationships. They talk about their fears, their hopes for the future, their fantasies. Since early childhood women have learned to be attentive listeners and good givers and this is evident in their friendships where they can give each other support, understanding, comfort, sympathy and advice. A woman gets a new job and she reaches for the telephone to tell her dearest friend; a woman discovers that her husband is having an affair and she reaches for the telephone to unload her distress with her friend; a woman wants to have an affair herself and reaches for the telephone to consult her friend about whether she should or shouldn't.

Women friends boost each other's confidence and

help to smooth out the difficult emotional details of daily life. They discuss the inevitable problems and worries they have about their kids, they live through the pleasurable and obsessive details of planning and executing family functions. Women look after each other's children, help in the preparation of parties, go shopping together for food and clothes, discuss various aspects of their working lives. For many women, intimate relationships with women-friends, sisters, aunts and co-workers are a bedrock of stability in their lives. The emotional texture of women's friendship is woven into the fabric of their daily lives. Indeed, *a woman without a best friend is a very lonely woman*. There is an exquisite intimacy to female friendship, the sharing of experience, of daring, of pain, of challenge.

A deep friendship with a woman provides a sense of continuity. Unlike lovers and husbands, friendships may well survive the tumult of changing sexual partnerships which is so common today. But at the same time, friends are used to fading in and out of the forefront of relationships. Friendship offers a different kind of security from that in a sexual relationship. Friendship implies an unstated acceptance, frequently missing in love affairs and marriage where the threat of the other leaving (or leaving oneself) often lurks somewhere on the agenda. What distinguishes women's friendships is the easy reciprocity that envelopes the relationship, allowing so many things to be safely discussed and felt.

Such is the positive, nurturing side of women's relationships. Women cooperate and support each other, and give each other enormous pleasure. But women's positive feelings towards each other have a counter point in equally powerful negative feelings. Women's relationships produce a rainbow of powerful emotions. The recent delight and recognition of the importance of women's relationships and the ideology of 'sisterhood is powerful' has, in some ways, served to obscure much of the pain in women's friendships. But as we can trust the

18

importance and value of these relationships, we are then able to face the fact that they are not idyllic. The relationships have the capacity to produce feelings of hurt and anger, envy and competition, guilt and sorrow. As women have been finding out to their great cost, close friendships, work collaborations, and entire organizations can be disrupted, even destroyed by unexpected negative feelings. When such painful feelings emerge in a work situation, or friendship, they can cause havoc and distress. The intensity with which they are experienced can be almost unbearable. And yet, equally as unbearable (or unthinkable), is the thought of talking directly to one's friend about the upset. For, within women's relationships, there is not yet an accepted context for talking about anger or hurt as there is within a marriage. And although many women may find it difficult to confront their sexual partners with critical or disturbing feelings on a regular basis, there usually comes a point when an explosive fight allows for the expression of them. Often within a couple relationship women find an outlet for their anger or hurt through indirect means – by withdrawing sexually, for example. Or perhaps a woman can 'take the liberty' of being in a bad mood, crabby and down with her partner, in an effort to indirectly communicate that something is not right. Yet rarely do we act similarly with a friend. We may withdraw by not telephoning as frequently. But when we do meet up, nine times out of ten we have swallowed our upset, digested it in some all too familiar way, and carried on without ever having aired our feelings.

For several years a group of women, who had initially come together as students and then as lawyers to start a legal practice in Birmingham, limped along intimately on the barest of resources only to find out that their subsequent success caused internal organisational havoc. As the practice prospered and each week's payroll could be comfortably met, and projects could be pursued without the pressure of imminent financial collapse, differences between them became both more obvious and less easy

19

to tolerate. Just as, at Richmond College, success itself seemed to have bred unforeseen difficulties. In adversity the women could give each other unending support, discuss all the angles in a case and work late on preparing each other's briefs. But in the face of an apparently relaxed environment, they saw the emergence of competition for the 'interesting' cases and tussles over the use of the researcher's time. In short, individuals felt aggrieved in different ways so that, eventually, an extremely attractive and non-hierarchical practice dissolved, leaving the eight members of the group feeling bitter and disappointed. It seemed as though women couldn't work together, and an experiment in sisterly principles had degenerated into petty disputes, time keeping and backbiting. Part of what made it impossible to keep the group practice together was the distaste and shock many felt on realizing the strong negative reactions which arose. Warmth was replaced with suspicion, sisterliness with competition and envy, generosity of spirit with feelings of meanness and anger. But could it all have turned out differently? What could these women have done to save their organization and the important relationships within it?

Often women's feelings of anger, betrayal, envy and competition towards one another occur most acutely in one to one relationships. Almost every woman is aware of at least one occasion in which, sitting with a friend who is telling her of some good fortune, she is startled to discover that she feels uncomfortable.

A woman may feel she is going to scream, cry, or reach over and shake her friend when that friend tells her she is pregnant. To be sure Julie, the drama teacher, was delighted for her friend Wendy. That wasn't the point. For ages Wendy had wanted to have a baby. For three years she'd been actively searching for a partner with whom to start a family and, once having married Tom, she had been trying to get pregnant for the year they had been together. But Julie was – to herself – unaccountably envious. She didn't want Wendy to be telling her she was happy. She didn't want Wendy to be bubbling about midwives and doctors and baby's names. She didn't want Wendy to be pulling her in and discussing when she should stop work, how it was affecting her sex life, how tired she was and how much she was eating. Julie wanted a baby herself. She wanted a different man and a job she liked and a new baby. She had a man she didn't like, a boring job and a teenage daughter who was causing her grief. She felt she'd had a baby far too young and ached to be in a situation where she could have a baby now, with the benefit of a maturer insight and understanding. All around her friends were having babies and feeling hopeful. She envied their energy and their enthusiasm. They all seemed capable of taking on so much and getting what they wanted.

Soon the pain of envy would be so difficult for her to bear that she would not return Wendy's calls and would see her less frequently. Was the slipping away of this friendship unavoidable? What could Julie have done with her feelings of envy?

One response employed by many women is to try to hide them. Joanna, a potter, bore the pain of her envy privately. Her best friend Jenny, who'd been living with her lover Mary for five years, had finally successfully conceived through artificial insemination. Now it seemed, Jenny had everything going for her – a nice home, an interesting job in the media, a relationship and a baby on the way. Joanna felt stuck in her work, couldn't seem to meet the men she wanted to and was approaching forty without the chance to decide whether or not she would be a mother. When Jenny announced her pregnancy Joanna gave her no hint of envy, bar a slight blush when it was first mentioned. She helped out with babysitting, knitted a few special jackets for the baby and was solicitous and kind during the pregnancy. But inside she was deeply jealous. Although she longed to have a baby, she didn't feel she should burden Jenny with her frustration. The most she could do was share her upset about everyone else having babies. On the outside she bore her envy of Jenny with dignity. On the inside she was in agony. But surely bottling up these distressing feelings can't be the only way to preserve a friendship?

The upset and envy which Julie and Joanna felt are not isolated instances. Increasingly we hear the angst of women in their late thirties and early forties who are facing a reality they did not predict. A generation of women have directed themselves towards self-development in areas outside the traditional role of wife and mother and, although their working lives may be fulfilling, they can no longer put off the decision of whether or not to have children. For some the circumstances of their lives combined with their age have made the decision for them. Many women have a deep desire for children but they are not with a partner; for others who are perhaps in couple relationships, the desire itself brings conflict. They feel ambivalent and find themselves weighing the pros and cons of having a child, the gains and the losses. This ambivalence can feel paralysing and yet they are terrified of the biological clock which refuses to stand still.

The decision of whether or not to have children is not uniform for this generation of women, which means women are continually confronted by friends, colleagues, relatives who are pregnant and having children. As a result there is an epidemic of powerful and deeply distressing feelings in women's relationships regarding pregnancy and childbearing. This is not to say that motherhood is the only source of envious feelings amongst women today. Envious feeling can be fuelled by other 'big' issues such as whether or not one is in a sexual relationship or whether or not one has a satisfying and well paid job. These feelings can erupt for what may appear to be much less 'significant' reasons.

Friendship in adversity, unity in the face of opposition, has been one of the hallmarks of the positive side of women's relationships. The difficulties that can occur when women or women's groups do well (and not badly), or the upset that is unleashed when differences surface in a relationship built on shared suffering, are realities women are now beginning to grapple with, in an attempt to understand themselves better and save valuable relationships. But they are realities often easier to ignore than to confront.

To understand how this has happened, we need to understand how the change in women's social role is affecting women's relationships. Alongside the gains of self-development, new areas of difficulties, new conflicts and new sorrows are emerging. We need to provide ourselves with a social and psychological perspective that can account for these changes. And we need to go further. We need to see the ways in which women are wrestling with these new realities, with the difficulties now arising, in one to one relationships, in women-run work settings, in business and professional contexts. Women have become accustomed to relying on each other for the fulfilling of many different needs. They have enjoyed the intimacy that exists in their relationships. The strengths in those relationships, combined with an accurate analysis of the present situation, will allow us to confront the difficulties, so that we can resolve them and move these crucial relationships forward.

CHAPTER 2

New Expectations

Whether or not one felt oneself to be a part of the Women's Liberation Movement, few in Western society today remain untouched by its ideas and demands. We have all been witness to one of the most radical decades of change for women this century. In many ways, ideas which at one time seemed drastically revolutionary have been incorporated into the very fabric of our homes, workplaces, school and art. Images of the bra burning, man-hating feminist have faded and in their place we see a woman with briefcase in hand putting in a hard day's work at the office, an exercise work-out scheduled into her busy day and coming home to a liberated dish-washing husband and the kids; or a woman with a hard hat and work boots, skilled in a trade that is new terrain for her gender. It is unclear and perhaps irrelevant to ask whether these women consider themselves to be feminists. They are just modern women living the lives they have come to expect for themselves and which are expected of them.

Indeed, women today are faced with a barrage of contradictory images of femininity. Women are executives; women are mothers; women are independent; women are weak and dependent; women are secretaries; women are engineers; women are sexually confident and liberated; women are loose and whorelike; women wear spiked high heels; women wear men's style shoes;

women wear silk teddies and lacy stockings; women wear tailored suits; women use their own American Express cards; women are doing the laundry and driving the children around; women pay housekeepers to do that work for them; women are other women's house-keepers. The list is endless but its meaning is clear. Women today are living in the heart of a social tornado. We've uprooted the old definitions which imprisoned us and we struggle to find our new and rightful place in the world outside as well as inside the family. We are strad-dling two worlds.

Newspapers and magazines announce that the women's movement is over, that the struggle for equal-ity is won. But women have learned that achieving status in the workplace, with all the discipline and ambition that entails, while at the same time remaining committed wives and loving mothers, is often unbearably deman-ding. And the media, ever hungry for new markets and new stereotypes, have compounded the pressure by surrounding us all with images of the new Superwoman who not only has a loving husband, a spotless home and cared-for children, but also a high paying, high powered career. The enormous stress that these new expectations cause is becoming obvious as the heart attack and lung cancer rates go up amongst women.

Where are we to get the strength to be today's Super-women? Those of us who were involved at the beginning of the women's movement gathered strength from shar-ing our common experiences. It broke down emotional isolation, and we found courage in our connection with each other. Where there was only one woman there were feelings of inadequacy, self-hate, passivity, fear. When she connected with others in a group there was revela-tion, understanding, empathy, rage, pain, unity, and a new sense of power. We began to look at other women differently, as people we could value, and in so doing we began to value ourselves. We were being transformed on an individual and social level.

Are women today still getting that same strength from

each other's support? Perhaps the greatest conflict women are facing today as a result of the movements' explosive impact is the crisis in their relationships with one another. As we have seen in Chapter 1, women are capable of achieving intimate relationships and deep friendships with one another. Recently, books have appeared which tell us of the need for us to honour friendships and to recognize that men have something to learn from women in this area. Feminist theoreticians have pointed to women's capacity to connect, to give, to relate intimately and the need for our society to value these feminine qualities. Women's role as nurturer and mother has always provided them with the skills and opportunities to relate and to not be frightened of emotional connection. Long before the women's movement, women achieved deep and significant friendships. Mothers and daughters, sisters and aunts, friends and neighbours relied on one another for practical and emotional support. Then, through the women's movement women's connection to one another deepened still further. As women revealed their most private thoughts and experiences they broke through to new levels of intimacy. Nothing had to be hidden. Women talked about the most personal details of their sexual lives and fantasies, they exposed what went on behind the scenes in their marriages and relationships both with men and other women. No area was *verboten*.

But something has changed. In our practice we hear women talk about new issues which they dare not discuss with their closest women friends. There has been a post-feminist, self-imposed censorship on certain feelings which women have determined as unacceptable. Feelings, for example, of competition and envy, are rampant. No woman today escapes them, but every woman is in conflict over them. Feelings such as these are the cause of tremendous pain and confusion for many women. There is a feeling of isolation. This isolation is not identical to the old isolation, though. It is similar in that, just as before, women are experiencing self-doubt, self-blame, inadequacy, envy of other women. Only this time around the conflicts are more complex. There are stronger forces at odds.

During the height of the women's movement, as we moved from a position of isolation to one of *camaraderie* with other women, our sense of entitlement grew. We knew we were fighting to open doors that had been closed to our mothers. When we walked through those newly opened doors we did so with great trepidation. In contrast to our mothers, many of whom had worked for economic or personal need, we had a sense of a movement behind us. The movement was our security blanket – we could have it with us as we took new and scary steps out into the world.

This world was one which men had occupied for centuries. Ours was supposed to be the home while theirs was the marketplace, and now here we were in foreign territory. Women had been here before, but in far fewer numbers and in a different way. They had been seen as the exceptions to their gender, unwomanly. As a movement we proudly and loudly announced ourselves as *women* before our arrival, and we were met with an array of responses. We were teased when we insisted upon being called women instead of girls but we persisted and we were called women. We gritted our teeth as male colleagues and bosses purposefully, or unconsciously, undermined our efforts and confidence, as they examined our work with fine-toothed combs, ready to jump on us for the tiniest of mistakes. While other male colleagues, aware of the powerful movement from which we'd come, recognized the contribution to be made, and revealed their more progressive discomfort by relating to women with a kind of awe or reverence.

The fact of the matter was that, although on one level we had a movement behind us, on a day to day level we were in those jobs on our own. Each woman had to meet the challenge of her particular circumstance and, in order to survive, she had to find her way in the foreign land of the masculine work world. She had to 'learn the ropes' –

working doubly hard to prove her competence. She had to adapt to the rules of the game in order to get in and stay in. She was entering an environment which had a history and a very particular ethos of competition – an ethos often at odds with the ethos of what it had previously meant to be a woman. It is a world in which rules of deference and rank are clearly defined and one does not dare to expose vulnerability or compassion, for fear of losing one's place on the ladder to promotion. In this new, unemotional world, the bonds between women are broken. In the world of every-woman-for-herself, the old support systems can be tragically undermined.

Ann Russell, a senior executive of a major publishing house is an extremely successful woman. A robust, warm and convivial woman of fifty-seven, she began her career as an editor when her second child started kindergarten. She soon became a senior editor, and four years later was promoted to Editorial Director. Throughout each of those promotions she was friends with a group of women colleagues. When Ann became Editorial Director, there was a noticeable shift in her relationship with her friends. Both she and they kept up lunch dates but they were less frequent. When Ann was promoted to senior executive, the change was even more noticeable. For the first month or so she was too busy adjusting to her new work responsibilities to arrange a date with her friends in editorial. As the weeks went by the distance between them increased. One day she was out to lunch with an author when she noticed all three of her old women friends at another table, sharing stories about their day, their home lives, their latest shopping trip, a new book or film. Her heart sank and she felt utterly desolate. She was an outsider, no longer a part of the group. The mere fact of her success had cut her off from them. Ann lived with a loneliness she had never before experienced at work.

Ann's 'success story' is not uncommon these days. In our practice we are increasingly hearing about the problems women experience in their relationships with other women, as they become more successful in their careers. Clearly Ann was paying a high price for her success. But why? Is this price inevitable?

Over the past decade more and more women have achieved a status that, previously, had been for men only. Competence on the job is not a concept women have imprinted in their understanding of what it means to be a woman. In the past, images of successful women have been more usually linked with glamour than professional efficiency. Where forceful women have been centre stage they have often been de-feminized, making it hard for the ordinary working woman to identify with her. It cannot have escaped our attention that the three women leaders of the 70s and 80s, Golda Meir, Margaret Thatcher and Indira Ghandi were all involved in wars – the ultimate masculine activity. Thus women in the public eye are often a long way from the role models ordinary women might wish to emulate. But, now that women are anticipating being in work contexts for many more years, seeing work as a place from which they derive crucial aspects of their identity, they are increasingly confronted with female superiors who they may wish to emulate or surpass. There are, for the first time in significant numbers, female bosses. This is a new kind of relationship for women, not always easy to negotiate. Women superiors cannot help taking on the mantle of role model, whether or not they set themselves up in this way. And for those on the way up, the feelings of competition and envy, the scurry for approval, the wish to be acknowledged and noticed by other women, are now a part of their daily office lives. These emotions can be troubling, and confusing, and often lead to real problems at work, which in turn affect women's new sense of self.

Elaine was an editor at Ann's publishing house. She had a list of lucrative authors and was accustomed to dealing with contracts involving large amounts of money. She, herself, had brought in two best sellers which made her company a great deal of money. Her own salary did not reflect the kind of contribution she made to the company and yet she was extremely nervous about asking for a raise. She alternated between feeling grateful that she had a good position and feeling furious that her contribution was not being financially rewarded. In addition, she was angry at herself, reflecting that a man in her position would hardly be acting this way. Although she didn't realize it at first, central to her passivity in seeking a raise was the effect on her of having a female executive – Ann – above her, who she would need to approach to ask for a raise. She felt Ann should recognize her contribution to the company and reward her without prompting. She felt Ann should 'know' how she felt. Somehow she felt that if she had to *tell* Ann she deserved a raise, maybe she didn't really merit it after all.

It took Elaine months to pluck up the courage to discuss a raise with Ann, and when she did it was in the most mealy mouthed way, trembling inside. Elaine got the raise she asked for. Six months later there was an office reorganisation and a man in the company was made responsible for personnel and salary decisions. Elaine had had yet another best seller and felt she had been too timid when asking for her last raise. She found herself one day in her new boss's office asking for an increase, without even having prepared herself for it. She was surprised by her forthrightness and as she left the room, raise negotiated, she reflected on how differently she had acted compared with six months earlier. She could hardly put it down to confidence arising out of that previous encounter, nor to any particular kindness on this man's part. The only thing that could account for the difference in her was that he was a man, while her previous negotiation had taken place with a woman. What this meant and why she felt insecure in front of a woman, and confident in front of a man, perplexed her. It was the exact opposite of what she imagined would have been the case. It was as if displaying her confidence to another woman was dangerous somehow, forbidden.

The admiration of women in positions of power can result in them being placed on a pedestal by other women. Once there, the woman principal, the professor, the account executive, the head buyer, the senior administrator, the doctor and so on, becomes the recipient of a range of feelings from those other women. Sometimes a female superior is seen as an enabling and inspiring figure, in that she has shown that a woman can succeed. But just as often the inspirational aspect gives way to feelings of jealousy, of anger, of wanting what that woman has. The successful woman becomes the focus of enormous amounts of interest and gossip. Her private life and her work actions assume proportions out of kilter with their actual importance. She becomes a figure of fascination and interest to those around her. A woman placed in such a position can become extremely isolated. Other women cease responding to her woman to woman; instead she has to relate through a quagmire of projections and fantasies. When she casually shares some vulnerability with a colleague, the colleague may be stunned, not imagining that her boss could possibly feel that way. It is as if, in being in a position of authority, of power at work, she is no longer a woman.

But even in women-run businesses, which have less of a clearly masculine orientation, less masculine work styles, we are now coming across situations in which psychological themes common to women appear. These produce new problems at work which have to be tackled if these women's enterprises are to continue to be successful.

Rita, a black New Yorker, was employed as a PA to the boss of a small interior design firm. She was a year older than her boss, less well educated in a formal sense but full of energy and spunk. The job gave her plenty of scope to expand from administration into making presentations to clients and selling her ideas. She'd been attracted to the job because it had the potential to be what she made it. Her boss 'Margaret' chose her because she seemed talented and able, had a good sense of humour

31

and promised plenty of initiative. But when she actually started working, Rita was less happy with how the job was going than might have been expected. As she put it, she 'underperformed' and did not really take advantage of the opportunities offered to her. Margaret felt the same way and regretted that Rita contributed less than they might both have wished. On the job, they had a companionable relationship, but why couldn't the wonderful collaboration they'd both wanted come to be?

In her therapy Rita talked about how incompetent she felt around Margaret and how she felt she was always concealing her shortcomings, and expecting to be found out. She admired Margaret greatly and had really aspired to being like her. When she first came to work for her she dreamt of making a good enough contribution so they could become partners. She was impressed with Margaret's confidence and saw it as real and solid, as opposed to her own which she felt was very superficial, shaky and somewhat of a put on. She wanted what Margaret had and part of her attraction for this job was the hope that Margaret could give it to her.

In reality, Margaret's confidence was almost as fragile as Rita's. Although her company was successful she was quite scared of expansion. Hiring Rita with such an open job description was a way of fudging the direction she should go in. She was unwilling to give the kind of leadership that would allow herself, Rita and the company to grow. Although she projected the knowledge and competence that an upper class education gave her, she was the first woman in her family to actually work for money and take that work seriously. She enjoyed both the actual design work and the contact with clients, but she couldn't conceive of herself as an employer who was building an expanding company.

Rita needed direction from Margaret and was disappointed and confused when she did not receive it. She continued to hold Margaret in some awe and to see her as perfect. She liked Margaret's easy going attitude, and she envied the relaxed way in which she ran her business. But to Margaret this attitude was a symptom of her own lack of ambition. She saw it as an expression of timidity, a failure to take advantage of the business opportunity she had created, and she felt guilty towards Rita whom she felt she was failing. Both women had expectations of Margaret that Margaret was unable to meet. Rita dealt with these by blaming herself and putting Margaret on a pedestal. Margaret dealt with these by blaming herself too. Their need to hide their insecurities from each other undermined the authenticity of their relationships and sabotaged the success of their collaboration.

Women's greater involvement in the workplace has affected their relationships outside it as well. Women find themselves engulfed by work commitments, preoccupied with issues related to work and with a driving energy which propels them to be more ambitious. Women who have partners or children find that, between work and family, little time and energy are left for their friendships with other women. Relationships which at one time seemed so central to daily life have faded, drifted away, hung together by a thin thread or ended. Even the memory of how these relationships made us feel, how they fed us emotionally and allowed us to be our own person, separate from our mates, has faded.

Eve comes home from her job at British Telecom at six o'clock, greets her two young children and husband and sits down to the chaotic accounts of each person's day. Her husband, Tom, quickly mentions that she got a phone call from her best friend Andrea and carries on to tell her about a talk he had with his boss. Her daughter shows her a book review she wrote at school that day at the same time as her son tries to tell her about the happenings at his dentist's appointment. She wonders if she'll manage to call Andrea back and is resentful that a phone call to her dearest friend should feel like yet another pressure. She's exhausted from a long day's work, but makes a great effort to be attentive to her family. She knows the children are extremely demanding because they haven't been with her all day, and they want and need a lot from her. She uses all her self-control to keep from screaming at everyone to shut up.

All she needs is a little peace and quiet, a few moments to relax and unwind. She knows she can't have that. She and her husband get dinner together, they all sit down to eat. After dinner her husband cleans up while she baths and prepares the children for bed. By 9 p.m. the kids are asleep and Eve collapses onto the sofa. She thinks about Andrea, her friend of 12 years. Earlier in the day she had thought about how she wanted to make a date to see her, something they try to do regularly – only regularly has lengthened over the years. It used to be at least once a week, with a phone call everyday – now for each of them with work and family – it was an effort to meet once a month. Eve summons up all the energy she's got left and goes to the phone. They speak for a few minutes commiserating about their exhaustion, filling each other in on a few recent developments and say they must make a date. They get their diaries and turn from one weekly page to the next in an effort to come up with an evening that's good for both of them. Between work related appointments, meetings, and family commitments, the date must wait nearly three weeks. With frustrated resignation they say good-bye and promise to speak again in a couple of days.

Each woman in her own way has had to adjust to the new demands the modern woman's life puts on her. One of the great rewards of the success of the Women's Liberation Movement has been the ability of women to be freer in their choices of when, how and if they have families. On the other hand, this freedom has led to a diversity that is not always easy to bridge. We saw in Chapter 1 how painful it was for Julie to learn of the news of Wendy's pregnancy. In our practice we increasingly hear women talk about their loneliness and their reluctance to 'intrude' upon a friend's life, particularly if one woman is single and the other involved with family. Single women with children have the additional stress of being single-parents, as well as finding many of their coupled friends unavailable to them. Whereas the coupled woman may emotionally depend upon both her partner and friends, the single women may have only her friends to rely on for a close relationship. The women upon whom she relied so strongly a decade ago, seem immersed in pregnancies, kids, partners and work.

Single and divorced women may feel the lack of female friendship much more acutely than women in families. Alison is thirty-three. She recently separated from her husband, Jack, and has been painfully adjusting to the break-up and to living alone. Her two closest friends are married. The women had been a threesome from their early twenties and had been through many ups and downs together. New men came and went but the 'girls' were always there. As they each got married their relationships with one another adjusted to their new lives. The women brought the men into the group and the couples spent a lot of time together. Since Alison and Jack split up she's seen them less frequently. Many nights when Alison returns from work she experiences anxiety upon entering her flat. Some nights it is more severe than others, but each time she desperately feels the need to phone someone, to make contact, to feel less alone. For the first couple of months after Jack moved out Alison felt it was alright to phone one of her two friends. They understood what a difficult time she was going through. But after several months Alison began to feel she could no longer call them so freely. She knew that they were each tired from a day's work and needed to relax with their husbands. She could hear their exhaustion in their voices and sensed they didn't have enough energy left to take care of her. She imagined they were beginning to feel annoyed with her. She sat alone in her flat, pained and upset.

Even when there are no concrete differences like work and families between women, the new expectations of today's women, the fantasies and projections of themselves and others, can form a barrier to friendship.

Marilyn and Angela work in the same occupational therapy unit. Both of them had considerable difficulty emotionally meeting the demands of their job. Both of them yearned for a good friend to confide in, but their images of each other got in the way.

Marilyn is forty-eight, married for twenty-six years, and the mother of three grown up children. She returned to university to get a post-graduate degree in occupational therapy when her youngest was in secondary school. When she got her first job she was thrilled beyond belief. After 20 years of being at home raising children and three long hard years at university she was finally entering the workforce in her own right. Her husband, Alan, and their youngest son who still lived at home had to adjust their schedules to hers. They all had to discuss who was going to shop for dinner and who would be home earliest to prepare it. The picture had changed dramatically. No longer was everyone else in the family out, while Marilyn maintained the homefront. Now she, like them, had another dimension to her life.

When she got her first paycheque she felt as if she had just won the Nobel prize. She had discussions with her husband about how each of their salaries would be used, knowing she wanted to maintain a substantial portion of hers for personal use. Earning a wage and having a job outside the home seemed to create a snowball effect in Marilyn's life. She found she was in a position to make decisions about various things on her own, when previously she would have felt obliged to check with Alan first.

For Marilyn the move from being a housewife to having a job outside the home gave her a profoundly new sense of herself as a person. She rediscovered parts of her personality that had lain dormant for decades. Marilyn felt a vitality and energy that she hadn't felt in years.

But the process of internal change, change of one's

psychology, one's sense of self, is often excruciatingly slow. It goes without saying that Marilyn's new connection to her job had a forceful impact on her. But Marilyn was having to deal with change from two sides -- her change in relation to her home and family and her new responsibilities at work. She had to grapple with feelings of guilt towards her son and husband for her lack of ever-ready availability and for her tiredness at night. She would find herself doing the laundry at ten o'clock at night, or running frantically to shop for food during her lunch hour. Somewhere inside she knew these things were not essential and yet she could not stop herself from doing them. At work she struggled with her lack of confidence, as she gazed at colleagues in disbelief when they asked her opinion about a course of treatment. It took a long time for her not to feel she was playing some kind of game which was shortly to come to an end. When she agreed to deliver a paper at a conference of occupational therapists she couldn't sleep for a month. She was so anxious that she couldn't think of anything but the presentation and had nightmares about losing her voice or fainting on the platform. She looked at her younger colleagues, like Angela, and imagined that they felt infinitely more confident in themselves than women of her generation. She envied the ease with which these young women could be members of the world which used to be for men only. She couldn't imagine they suffered the same anxieties that women of her generation experienced. Younger women seemed to have an air of self-assuredness and entitlement. They were ambitious and didn't have to even think about having children until they reached thirty.

Meanwhile Angela has her own feelings of insecurity and her own fantasies about who Marilyn is and what she feels. Angela went to post-graduate studies directly after finishing her BA. She had become interested in occupational therapy in college when her favourite aunt suffered a nervous breakdown and was helped by an occupational therapist during her stay in hospital. Like

Marilyn, Angela came from a working class family. Her father was a bus driver and her mother worked for the Electricity Board. She was the first in her family to go to university and into a white collar profession. Although she knew she did her job well, she was still riddled with feelings of fraudulence in relation to her co-workers. Her own words would echo in her head when she spoke to someone on a professional basis. It was almost impossible for her to feel she was a highly trained and qualified person. She carried her mother in her head and could not help feeling she was out of place in this world of sophisticated, middle-class people.

Angela imagined that, as an older woman, Marilyn felt confident and ripe from experience of the world. She gave her respect, as did other workers, both male and female, because she was older. Angela's unarticulated assumptions were that women of that generation didn't have to struggle with the awful decision about whether or when to have children. Marilyn had had her children and, now that she'd satisfied that part of herself, she had the freedom to concentrate on her career. She wasn't thirty and single and desperately watching the biological time-clock ticking by. She'd been married to the same husband for twenty-six years and didn't have to deal with the god-awful singles scene, looking for a man who doesn't exist.

Angela and Marilyn, despite their different ages, share more than they know. These women are situated at different spokes of the same wheel – the wheel of women's changing social role. Each spoke contains its own pressures of an internal and external nature. There are differences and there are similarities. A woman's age, her class, her sexuality and her race may place her on a different spoke in the revolution of the wheel, to which she brings varying expectations, restrictions, desires, and dreams. The emphasis of change has been on what she can be. But who she is, how she feels about herself, how she manages the new possibilities in her life, are greatly affected by the underlying sense of who she is as a woman in our society.

The kinds of changes that women have made over the past fifteen years have gone beyond a superficial level (who wears a bra and who doesn't), beyond a social level (who does the dishes) and into profound changes on the psychological level; profound changes in the very meaning of gender. Gender is not simply a matter of sex roles. Sex roles are a set of functions and activities, which are determined by any given culture, for the males and females within that culture. As a gendered person a girl or boy grows into a sex role. The challenge to, and change in, women's sex roles over the past decade has had an impact on women's internal sense of self. Girls and women continue to know themselves as feminine – that is, their gender has not become confused – but the *meaning* of femininity has changed.

Femininity is a deeply profound sense of oneself as of the feminine gender, as female. Hand in hand and inseparable from the development of a sense of self, of I, of a personality, is the sense of oneself as a gendered person. We come to know ourselves in the world as either feminine or masculine and gender is a primary structural building block within our personality, our psychology.

Obviously, femininity is not simply a matter of clothes or make-up. But historically, grooming and external appearance have been crucial aspects of how women have felt about themselves as women. It serves as an interesting paradigm for the changes in the meaning of femininity itself, to look at how women's attitudes to these external trappings of femininity have changed over the last fifteen years.

At the beginning of the Women's Liberation Movement, we rejected out of hand everything that we understood as society's definition of feminine. Although we may have called ourselves 'feminists', we sometimes seemed to accept the notion that 'feminine' had to mean weak, passive, unserious, and artificial. We wore masculine jeans and work boots and went 'natural', wearing no make-up, and no longer shaving our legs or our underarms; we took off our bras. It was as if we had to throw off the old dress to aid us in throwing off the old ways of being. And now we clung to the new code of women in ways not unlike the ways our mothers clung to the old code.

Having this new code, this new uniform, was important to us. It helped us to feel part of something. Being associated with the women's movement and being accepted by other women provided a sense of security that each woman yearned for. The movement itself symbolized a good mother who could be proud of her femininity, her womanliness, her strengths; a good mother who could encourage us to stretch ourselves and develop in areas where we had previously felt so prohibited and undermined; a good mother with whom we could identify and feel connected; a good mother who held out her arms to hold us, and have us be part of a loving, positive, secure, feminine, woman's world. Sisterly appreciation and love for other women was food for our own efforts towards self love.

The self-acceptance gained through our relationships with one another allowed for deeper feelings of self-confidence and those feelings, in turn, led to steps of autonomy. Women began to develop inner feelings of solidity, which could only have come from that first step of love and acceptance by other women. As each woman could feel secure in her attachment to other women she was able to feel more of her own person. From this more secure base she could risk moving towards further self-actualization, even if this took her out of the cocoon of women's (the new mother's) arms. Just as an infant, having first known itself through mother's reflection, moves on to develop a unique, independent and differentiated self, so too did women, full of other women's positive reflection and love, move on towards steps of differentiation.

Revealingly, as women started to differentiate, they started to let go of the rigid external uniform of early feminism. Surely, there were pangs of guilt as women shaved their legs or put on eye make-up. Did this mean we were backtracking? Did this mean that the movement was over and we were merely returning to the old ways of femininity? Not really. We were following an impulse, a desire which both helped us to be individuals within the movement, at the same time as it reconnected us with aspects of our mothers, whose lives we felt we had so profoundly rejected. In some ways our rejection of our mothers and their lives was being turned around, as our anger towards them changed to an understanding of their limits, of their lives as women just like us. We were unconsciously attempting a synthesis. After a decade of uncovering the old femininity, of criticizing its damaging and oppressive effects, of rejecting it and attempting new definitions, we needed to consolidate. We needed to chew over and digest all that we had taken in. Consciously we knew we had come a long way and that it was possible to .be a strong, self-loving, competent woman, who also shaved her legs or wore make-up. These traditional feminine characteristics did not have to be the sole determinants of who we were to be as women, as they had been in the days before the movement. Reclaiming the feminine as a part of us was another step in the evolution of women's sense of self. We no longer had to reject one code of femininity and adopt, *en masse*, an opposite code in order to be able to feel the strengths, the entitlement, the self-assuredness that we wanted to feel. Differentiating from other women, from friends, was a developmental step. By gaining the love of other women, we could love ourselves. By gaining the nurturing and permission from other women to move ahead, we were able to grow. We could allow ourselves to embody the femininity of our mothers, and generations of women before them, as we embodied the new images of womanhood which we were creating.

Although women's lives are still largely constrained, (and this is more emphatic depending on one's class or racial background) women today are freer to make more

41

choices in their lives than perhaps at any other time in history; choices about career, sex roles, sexuality, motherhood; choices about what it means to be a woman. The change, from a social role in which the mandate was connection to others, availability to others, self-defence and support for others, to a role which includes self-actualization, self-interest, entitlement and desire for a place in the world, as well as in the family, requires differentiation. And differentiation defies the very essence of feminine psychology. Prohibitions against women's autonomy and their position in the world outside the home as separate, effective, substantive people, are dynamic forces in this new crisis in women's relationships. Do we have to pay the price of having one or the other? That is, can we be people in the world without engendering envy or competitive and resentful feelings in our women friends? Do we have to lose the very people from whom we desparately need continued support? Have the recent changes in women's social position produced irreparable gaps in women's relationships with one another? We think not. But in order to bridge those gaps, we must come to a more profound understanding of the deep psychological meanings of women's attachments to each other.

1. Of course this is far from the truth. Women's economic position is not improving and while new vistas have opened up, equality at work and home is a long way off.

CHAPTER 3

Merged Attachments

How can we understand these two phenomena: the easy, comfortable and cosy feelings that women can create together and the difficult misunderstandings which can shatter those feelings? How is it that women feel the preciousness and importance of each other's support one moment and feel anger, envy and betrayal at another? What motivates women's desperate need for each other and their disbelief that they can have the acceptance they so want from one another? How can we understand the closeness between best friends and the bitter repudiation of that relationship when there is a falling out?

We put these questions together because there is a clash between women's positive feelings for one another and their difficulties with each other. Women's positive feelings for each other undoubtedly outweigh the problems that they are now encountering, but it is important to understand that the latter are not an aberration of the former, or a negation of them. Rather, it is the case that these feelings share the same roots. The developmental and social processes that are at the heart of women's easy connections are the *very same processes* that are at the heart of their difficulties with one another.

Sheila, a thirty-year-old illustrator is lunching with her friend Rosemary, who is also thirty, married and works in advertising. Most of the conversation centres on Rosemary's frustration over not getting pregnant; she's been trying for six months. As they get ready to leave the restaurant a woman with two small children walks in and sits down at the next table. Rosemary and Sheila smile at her in acknowledgement both of the cuteness of the kids and the awareness that the woman has her hands full. Sheila feels a pang of pain for Rosemary and senses this must have been a painful moment for her.

The pang Sheila felt is typical of the way in which women friends can feel so connected that, at times, it is as if one is in the other's shoes. This empathetic connection is a common feature of women's psychology. A woman's emotional tentacles seek out the precipices in life's emotional terrain. Her receptivity and responsiveness to that terrain feeds her and those around her and gives them an emotional base. Thus Sheila sensed Rosemary's pain. Without anything being said or indicated by Rosemary, Sheila was actuely aware that, for Rosemary, seeing young children was poignant. In her awareness Sheila actually *felt* pain. For a brief moment there were no boundaries between them, Sheila's heart was an extension of Rosemary's. During a silent moment they shared an intense communication.

In fact the three women – one a complete stranger – shared a similar connection just moments before. As they exchanged glances there was a complex communication which said "We know the pleasure you must feel with your two sweet children and we know the stress and pressure you feel in keeping this whole little scene together." The stranger felt understood, appreciated, proud, and supported by the two women at the next table.

Sheila and Rosemary not only saw the other woman's

situation but, for a split second, knew it as if from the inside. When Sheila and Rosemary left the restaurant, Sheila asked Rosemary if it was difficult for her to see other women with young children. The two friends, arm in arm, continued their caring and deeply intimate conversation.

Sheila, like other women, has developed emotional antennae. From early on in her life she was directed to be aware of the feelings and needs of others. Her experience of herself, when anyone else was around, was *Sheila* in relation to *other*. Knowing what someone else is feeling, without their needing to articulate it, was one of the first lessons she absorbed as a girl. The more finely tuned in she is to the needs of others, the more highly developed are her skills of intuition. Women's antennae allow them to set people at ease in their discomfort, avoid topics of discussion which cause embarrassment, blush as another person feels shame or humiliation, give a compliment to a near stranger that hits the right spot, tell a funny story when the social situation requires lightening up. Women's antennae provide social lubricant when it is required and a safety net for feelings which so often are out of our conscious control.

Our upbringing as girls prepares us to be receptive, to be giving, to be thoughtful, to be kind, to be solicitous, to take account of one another, to see things from the other person's point of view, to feel ourselves in another person's shoes. But these are not simple lessons we learn, like algebraic formulae or our times table, rather they are the grammar of women's emotional experience, the internal declensions that organise our relationships to others and to self. Within this language, we absorb that emotional grammar, the psychological laws of women's culture, which are every bit as explicit and particular as the cockney language is an encoded expression of the social heritage of London working class culture.

In absorbing the emotional imperatives that are to be women's way of being, we learn not only to be giving, intuitive, receptive, caring, empathetic, we learn too that

45

it is ungrammatical to be separate, initiating, autonomous and self-defined. These ways of being are not considered desirable in girls. Independence, adventurousness, a concern for self are not values that are proudly developed in girls. And those who grow up to be independent women are considered freakish in one way or another. They are seen as brash, as spinsterish, as sad, as selfish, as castrating. They evoke our sympathy or distaste. Their personalities are out of line with how we see femininity. We may admire the young woman surgeon for her confidence and ability, but if she devotes herself entirely to her work and remains single, by the time she is in her forties we may feel uneasy, threatened and somewhat perplexed. We assume that she is odd. Even if it is evident she is happy, and even if we defend her choices and are inspired by her courage, we can't help but feel some discomfort for her. For even today, while we are in the midst of expanding our ideas of what are appropriate behaviours and feelings for women, a woman who resolutely goes her own way jolts us. Deeply etched into our very identity are the grammatically correct ways of being (i.e. psychologically attached) and the grammatically incorrect ways of being (i.e. psychologically separate) women.

In short, girls grow up learning that to know what others want, caring for them and being attached to them is right and must be the way they organise their lives. They must create a selfhood dependent on this kind of connecting to others. Acting on one's own initiative and seeking a separate identity is wrong unless it comes second. This doesn't mean that girls and women aren't attracted to what is 'wrong' (for they are), it doesn't mean that girls and women don't desire autonomy and separateness (for they do), it means rather that their attempts to achieve it are extremely fraught, loaded with guilt and confusion.

Women's desire for love, acceptance and support from each other, is related in a complex way to the heritage and the potential we have experienced in our first relationship with a woman. For all of us raised in the Western style family today, the most significant relationship we have had, the relationship that birthed us physically and emotionally, the relationship in which we first felt love and need, the relationship in which we first felt disappointed and hurt, the relationship whose emotional legacy is etched in the deepest recesses of our hearts, is the relationship with mother.

This relationship is a foundation for the future. What occurs in it guides us in our forthcoming relationships. It sets up needs, ways of being, ways of loving, expectations and hopes. We have to examine that original mother-daughter relationship in order to understand its legacy. We have to understand what needs it made permissible, and what needs were made inadmissible. We have to understand the texture and feeling of it. We have to understand the particular, merged attachment, that characterised it, before we can grasp both the love and the disappointment, the hope and the hurt that exist in adult women's relationships.

The security we feel inside ourselves as individuals, the enthusiasm or fear with which we engage in new relationships, the possibilities we have imagined for ourselves and the life we have made for ourselves has much to do with what was experienced and conveyed in that first important relationship. And that very first relationship, from its inception, is both an enabling and a disabling one. It is a relationship that is characterised by merger. It is a relationship in which the attachment that occurs, which *both* mother and daughter experience, is both blissful and problematic.

The mother-child relationship is at once a private relationship and a relationship bearing public responsibility. It is the relationship that nourishes and protects us, while introducing us and preparing us for the social world. In this sense, infancy and childhood are not cosy stages divorced from the wider culture, but developmental stages shaped in accordance with the social practices of a given culture. In the very intimacy of the mother–

47

child relationship is the imprint of the social laws that mother must pass on to us. What a mother endeavours to prepare her daughter for, and what her mother tried to prepare her for, is to live in some degree of harmony as an individual and to take her place in the world.

The setting of the mother–daughter relationship in a social context is important, for it can begin to explain, not only the bittersweet nature of that relationship, but its impact on adult women's relationships. As we understand what could and could not happen for our mothers in their lifetime, as we understand what could and could not happen in our relationships with our mothers, we can begin to understand the forces operating in our current woman to woman relationships.

When we leave our mother's womb, we live in a cocooned state with her. Before the baby 'knows' itself as a person, with a distinct inside and outside, before it can distinguish itself from the people and objects around it, it exists in a merged state with mother. Just as, prior to birth, it lived within the actual boundaries of mother's body so, after birth, it lives within the mother's psychological boundaries. The mother sets up a psychological milieu that the two inhabit. To put it more precisely, the aspects of the mother that are preoccupied with caring for the infant, and the infant in its entirety, live within this psychological framework.

We tend to think of infancy in a romantic way. We imagine an enraptured mother with a baby at the breast. Developmental psychologists describe this as a time when a mother is 'given over' to caring for her baby. She feels herself into the baby's experience and, almost as though there were no membrane separating the two of them, she merges with the baby, feels what it wants in the way of holding, feeding, warmth and so on and effortlessly makes the necessary adjustments to maintain its well-being. She guides its psychological development from infantile dependency to subjectivity (separation–individuation[1]). The mother, as a separate person, with her own needs, distinct from the baby, is

48

not in view. She is only seen in this role as a person who perfectly meets the needs of her infant.

But this idealised picture of a mother, effortlessly responding to her baby's every wish and relating appropriately to the developmental stage, conceals a much more complex situation. For, however in tune a mother may be with her baby, the mothering person is also an individual with needs of her own. And this fact and her needs are not excluded from the mother-daughter relationship; they are brought to it and form a part of it.

Thus there is not a straightforward relationship between the sensing of an infant's need and responding to it. For the responses themselves are highly affected by the mother's emotional state of affairs; these are determined by the complex of economic, psychological and social circumstances in which she finds herself. The infant's needs and initiatives invariably evoke some complicated feelings in the mother, which lead to an inconsistency in the relating.

At times, each mother can respond selflessly to the needs and initiative of this little girl and she soothes, comforts, encourages, delights in and loves her effortlessly. The little girl shows her pleasure and her satisfactions, she beams back a smile, a look of contentment that gives the mother a good feeling about herself, which is re-reflected back and fourth between the two of them. But, often times, mother has difficulty with her daughter's expression of need and this easy relating is disrupted. The mother who continually restrains both her own needs for emotional nourishment and her own initiatives is unable to respond to her daughter in an open and generous way. Her responses to her child are characterised by annoyance and withdrawal. At these times the daughter feels confused and rejected. A chain reaction occurs in which, the child's need (whether it be for contact and holding or for support in showing independence) is being ignored, misinterpreted, mismatched by the mother's response in one way or another, creates in the daughter an insecurity and uncertainty about herself/her need.

The emotional ambiance of the merged attachment, then, contains these contradictory aspects. The relationship is at once the soothing, safe protective environment and the utterly disappointing, frightening, painful place where all can be lost. Mother who is caught up in her own internal drama, cannot help but respond inconsistently to her daughter's needs. The daughter, however, has to make sense inside herself of her mother's variable responses to her needs.

Of course this phenomenon, the inconsistency that occurs in the merged attachment, which leaves a child perplexed about what needs and initiatives are sanctioned and what needs and initiatives are not, is a feature of all mother-child relationships. But the character of the inconsistency, the particular shape of the inconsistency, is intimately related to the child's gender, and the way in which the mother sees herself in her child and identifies with the various needs the child is expressing. Mother sees a son and a daughter differently. Mother can see her son as 'other', as different, because of the gender difference between them. It represents a clear cut boundary between them. He is he and she is she. This use of gender to aid in differentiation is not present with a daughter. Throughout the many phases of her daughter's life mother watches and is continually reminded of her own girlhood. Pictures of her own childhood insinuate themselves into the interaction between her and her daughter. When she looks at her daughter she sees in her, her own childhood; her own childhood wishes, her own childhood desires as well as the restrictions she experienced. In other words, *she sees herself in her daughter.*

What are the psychological implications for daughters, of mothers' and daughters' shared gender? Mothers have most difficulty in sanctioning their daughters simultaneous needs for dependency and their needs to initiate. For, a critical social law that a mother passes on to her daughter, is that the development of the daughter's selfhood must take place in a relational context. Like her mother, she should find 'herself' and know 'herself' through responsiveness to others. Like her mother, she should curb her own needs for nourishment. Like her mother, she must limit her own initiatives, in so far as they interrupt her availability to others. Like her mother, she will come to understand that autonomy is not a route to feminine selfhood. Selfhood will be found through her identification and adjustment to the needs of others.

These social laws, which pass from mother to daughter, also occur in the mother–daughter relationship. For mother brings her needs into the relationship with her daughter.

Foremost of these is the mother's need for attachment. Women know themselves through their connections to others, in other words, a woman's subjectivity is relational. She has known herself in connection to, in the service of and for, others. She has no experience of an identity apart from this. Her connection to her child, like any other intimate connection, contains a crucial piece of her psychological selfhood. Mother brings this experience of self, and the urgency of *her* need for connection, into the relationship with her daughter. Thus the period of infantile dependency is marked, not only by the daughter's psychological merger and need of mother, *but with the mother's need for psychological merger with her daughter*. In bringing this need for merger and connection to her daughter, she parenthetically leaves her daughter with a sense that this is how she, too, will discover herself.

And just like mother, the daughter comes to have an incomplete sense of self which seeks affirmation through connection. Without the connection there is an underlying insecurity about one's very identity. For without connection, a feminine identity is at risk.

From very early on in the little girl's life, she is encouraged to take account of others' experience, to disregard and repress her own desires, to seek the satisfaction of her own needs in the meeting of needs in others; indeed,

51

to know herself through her attachments to others. Mother, and all those who relate to the girl, respond to and develop in her those capacities that will fit her psychologically for her future social role. Developing a separate identity and placing her own needs in the foreground are discouraged. Attachment to and concern for others become her guide. The daughter is taught to interpret her own feelings in this light. She begins to identify the satisfying of others' needs, and complying with others, as *a need of her own*. She develops the capacity to feel herself into others' experiences, to know what they are wanting and needing.

But her sensitivity to others' needs does not only come from the instructions she receives, to be watchful and solicitous. It is also because her own needs have gone unmet, or become distorted, that she becomes attuned to neediness in others. And it is out of her own deep neediness that a capacity is invoked within her which allows her, in turn, to identify with, emotionally register with and respond to the requirements of others.

This capacity to project herself into someone else's experience and the impulse to take account of others' feelings, which are such central features of woman to woman relating, at the same time render in her an insecurity regarding other kinds of emotions that arise in her. While she develops the expertise to heed the emotional needs of others she becomes curiously inexperienced and embarrassed by her own. Desires that surface in her such as a wish to be 'free', on her own, unencumbered by the emotional demands of others, that is, desires which signify a break with the merged attachment, confuse her. Desires for self nurturing, or desires that compete with her caring for others, perplex her, for she does not receive consistent or unambiguous support for them. They hang suspended in her personality and internally she juggles with them, at one moment repressing them at another seeking their open expression. Over time, she comes to be fearful of the wishes she may have to pursue her own initiatives. Desires she may

52

experience for autonomy, for separateness, frighten her. Because of this fear, she is unable to move out of the state of merged attachment, for it feels safe and known. It is as though she faces a dreadful choice. Either she can exist as a lone individual unconnected to others or she is trapped in a nexus of cloying attachments. She does not believe she can have both her attachments and her autonomy. She has no experience of this.

She has learnt directly and indirectly, in this first important relationship with her mother, that attachment to others – a prerequisite of survival – depends upon two features. (1) The repression of her own 'needing-to-be developed' selfhood and (2) an almost compulsive concern for others. Thus attachment, as she knows it, is itself problematic. For it is characterised by repression and merger. It goes hand in hand with the loss of a personal identity.

As we can see, the shared gender of mother and daughter, has many implications for woman to woman relating. The mother's need for attachment, combined with her identification with her daughter, creates a fusion between the two of them (a merged attachment). The mother is not separate from her daughter and, as her daughter expresses her needs, the mother experiences them *with* her, almost as though they were *her own*. She feels them too.

And as the daughter grows into womanhood she has an equivalent experience. Not only does she retain her mother's presence inside her, not only does she feel acutely aware of her mother's neediness, not only does she feel responsible for maintaining the attachment she feels her mother needs, but, unconsciously, she will bring this responsibility with her into her future relationships with both lovers and friends.

In adult relationships she is searching to find herself. But because the only mechanism she has for doing so is through merging and identifying with others, she comes to these relationships with emotional malleability. She comes with her emotional antennae ready to tune into the needs of the other. She is ready to adjust herself, deny herself, indeed lose herself (in order to find her 'self') in the attachment. But this process means that she loses sight of her own separate needs and desires. A search begins to find them in the other. She may no longer know what she wants, in a clear way, and looks to the other to provide an answer. She is dutifully concerned with the desires of her lover or friend, and gauges herself accordingly. She knows no other form of intimate attachment. Her adult relationships are woven with the threads of merged attachments.

But these threads are not simply connecting. They are constricting and binding. In the attachment, individual needs or individual development are a threat and so they are resisted. While the merger serves to shore up a shaky identity, it simultaneously precludes separate development. Thus an existence based on merger means that women are bound to one another in a restricting way. Without realising it, in bonding together to find strength, they severely limit one another.

This phenomenon of merged attachment is the fabric out of which adult female friendships are fashioned. Like a patchwork quilt, dark and light, patterned and plain, soft and rough materials play off one another creating an intricate whole. In the merged attachment, the different strands are composed of contradictory feelings, injunctions and longings. If we follow one piece of the pattern, we can see how women are able to intimately connect, to care for one another in the most exquisitely sensitive of ways. Another patch issues the injunction to relate to, and be in the service of, others. If we focus on another piece of the pattern we see how women unwittingly hold themselves and each other back; how their fear of separation leads them to sabotage their own efforts, and those of their dearest friends, towards autonomy. Indirectly and unknowingly, women restrain their friends; they discourage their efforts towards separateness and success. Through their fear of abandonment, or their threat to abandon one another, they let each other know that attempts towards separation are dangerous.

As we make out another pattern in the patchwork, we see how, with one another, women attempt to repair painful aspects of their relationships with their mothers, to alleviate the pain and disappointments they carry; to find a relationship that gives them love while allowing them to be separate. Close by, another patch shows the fear, the hesitation, the disbelief that they can have such a connection; that they will be allowed to be separate and still receive love and acceptance. As we focus on the different patches that make up the whole we see that *women's psychology is currently constructed in such a way that her capacities to be close and giving and her fear of separation are psychically inseparable.*

THE GIVER

Roberta is an administrative nurse in a large New York hospital. She is responsible for the services that go on for all post-operative patients in a particular wing. Doctors, other nurses, family members, general staff, all look to Roberta as the nucleus for information and organization. Her day is filled from early morning to early evening with people asking questions, giving instructions and information, relaying messages, solving problems which continually arise, and generally maintaining order. Everyone thinks Roberta is fantastic. She does her job so well that even in the hectic, frenzied pace, all who come into contact with her are aware of her competence, her concern, her dedication. The staff know that without Roberta the wing would dissolve into utter chaos. Roberta is single and lives alone. Most weekday evenings she returns home after work and eats her supper in front of the television. By the time she goes to bed she berates herself for not doing anything worthwhile and not keeping to her diet. On evenings when she goes out with a friend she enjoys listening to their news and commiserating or offering advice. She rarely talks about herself, but she enjoys the shared time and feels sustained by the contact and the knowledge that she has given something to her friend.

Roberta knows only too well how to be on the giving end of a relationship. She feels comfortable and safe. She gets satisfaction out of being able to accomplish the multitude of tasks at work and feels wise in her ability to 'counsel' her friends. We all know a Roberta, a woman who always has something to give and seemingly little need of her own. But does she truly have little need? What are Roberta's needs?

The truth of the matter is that Roberta's needs are there in the shadow of her giving. One need not look too far, or one will miss them. Just as a shadow follows immediately in the path of its object, so too are Roberta's needs connected to her giving.

A central feature in Roberta's giving is her own emotional hunger. She finds the exposure of anybody's need uncomfortable and she rushes to satisfy it. Each time she is presented with a person's need, be it little or big, her own neediness is touched. As she gives to the other, unconsciously she is attempting to satisfy her own unmet requirements. Part of her ability to know, to intuit, to read the needs of others comes from her own yearning for that very same care. Roberta does not feel entitled to bring her own needs to a relationship. She is ashamed of them and afraid of her insatiability. She has no confidence that she (and her needs) have a beginning and an end. It is as though she has no boundary, no knowledge of a defined self. This is the 'cost', the damage of living in the shadow of others and being such a good giver. Although she gives all the time, she is continually in retreat from a friendship to which she can bring her inner self. She is disabled in her relationships with others.

Roberta, like others, learned from very early on, to curb her own neediness. As we have seen, her own self-development was channelled towards the care of others and the search for her own 'self' in others. When little girls make demands on their own behalf they are often met with disapproval. The little girl's wants are seen to be selfish and unattractive. In an attempt to hide her demands, whether they be for individuality and initiating, or for cuddling and containment, a part of a girl's developing personality becomes buried. We have come to call this buried part the little-girl inside each woman. Outwardly the woman appears to be a person who can stand on her own two feet, be competent in the world, be the person on whom others can depend both emotionally and physically. And indeed she is. But inside exists that part of her which still longs for continued attachment. She has come to dislike and fear this part of herself which continually reminds her that she, too, has needs.

Part of women's psychological legacy, in being delegated to the position of caretaker of others and having been denied the essential foods for her own self-development, is that many a woman comes to feel an emptiness inside. Her emptiness is linked to the inconsistency of caring she has received which creates a sense of emotional deprivation. This emotional deprivation often translates as compulsive giving, depression, hopelessness, chronic resentment or rage. When she is in the presence of others she spontaneously gives them attention and responds to their needs. Looking after others in this way feeds her and keeps her going and gives her a good feeling about herself. Roberta is perhaps an extreme example of someone who finds it very hard to reveal that she has needs. Indeed, she may not even be conscious of her own needs, except in times of crisis when they are forced to the surface. She is deeply ashamed of them and unused to addressing them directly. The only hint she gives others and herself is her preoccupation with weight and dieting, for in that arena she can talk about how unhappy she is and how 'out of control' she feels around food. But most of the time, as she sits with a friend or a lover, feeling vaguely unsatisfied, she may be too cut off from even realising how much she yearns for them to reach out to her, to see inside her, to accept her neediness, to understand it and to give to her. When she is in crisis and people do rally around her, she can feel humiliated and hate herself for exposing what seem like unreasonable needs.

Roberta's story is not that uncommon. It is part of the legacy of our upbringing that creates in us both the capacity to care and a fear of our own needs.

The closeness of another woman in adult friendships stimulates and recreates the desire for a merged attachment. For in this merged attachment a woman finds a 'self'. But equally the little-girl inside longs for a different kind of attachment, an attachment which will acknowledge her past needs, the restrictions she has experienced and address her present needs. For if these needs were to be addressed, the little-girl inside could mature. The woman would no longer feel desperate and insatiable. Her personality would not have to be split, but could become integrated. She would develop a more secure subjectivity. A sense of selfhood based on *having* rather than one based on the experience of deprivation. A sense of selfhood based on entitlement rather than denial. A sense of selfhood that is contained rather than compulsively relational. While it is not possible to do away with the hurt of our childhood, it is possible to acknowledge and understand that hurt. In being able to come to grips with it, it becomes possible to use the nurturance that is available in our present relationships more effectively. As we can acknowledge the pain, the hurt and the disappointment of the past; as we can accept that it wasn't 'our fault' that we didn't get what we felt we wanted and needed, so current and future relationships need not be exclusively burdened by the need for either repair or replay of the past. They can be relationships between equal adults who both have needs, rather than paradigms of mother-child relationships in which one is the apparent giver and the other, the apparent receiver.

But this is the precise area of difficulty for women, for we have little confidence that relationships and a selfhood not built on a version of the mother-child merger (in which the compulsive attending to needs of the other, the repression of one's own initiatives and the denial of difference are endemic) can survive.

If we explore the implications of our analysis, we can see that at times a woman's identification with the needs of the other matches the other's experience, but often it does not. When it fails to, it is because a woman's malleable boundaries create confusion about where she ends off and another person begins. This interferes with appropriate relating. A particular kind of giving is occurring. Often in projecting oneself into the other's shoes, one misinterprets the other's experience. In identifying, one actually puts oneself in the place of another. This is an unconscious process. Identification is used in the search for a self. Women's capacity to identify is almost automatic. As we listen to a woman friend telling us about a problem or dilemma we *feel* with her. It is as though it were happening to us. This kind of emotional response, this capacity to feel what another is feeling, in short, our identification, is second nature. But, while it appears to bring us closer to one another, it simultaneously distorts the contact.

Because of women's psychological history, because of the nature of the mother–daughter merged attachment, because of the intensity of need that is brought to women's friendships with one another, women often fall into an experience of identifying with one another rather than seeing objectively the other's experience and empathising with it. In other words, for many women there is a confusion between empathy and identification.

Empathy and identification, though similar, contain an important difference. Empathy is the ability to imagine or think about another person's condition or state, taking on the feelings of the other only fleetingly. Empathy is a conscious process, in the sense that one is attempting to understand the experience of the other. One remains detached and outside the situation, at the same time as one may be deeply involved with the other person in the process of relating.

The ability to feel empathy provides a woman with a

most valuable skill to bring to friendships, to parenting, to intimate relationships. The ability to be with other people authentically – that is, to see them as they are, who they are in their own right, to respond to what they need and not to see them as we need or imagine them to be – is no easy feat. For it depends on an awareness of self as a unique, defined, autonomous individual, who relies and depends upon connections to other separate, defined, autonomous people.

As we have seen, women's facility to connect occurs in an emotional field that has both negative and positive currents. While one current surges with our craving for love, for understanding, for recognition, for sympathy, for support, for commiseration from one another, it is entwined with another wire which binds us with a negative charge. The negative wire disrupts those apparently easy connections by emitting a whole set of interferences – a constricting field of social and psychological mandates through which women prohibit one another from certain kinds of self-expression. The combined currents create the texture of the relationship and the often unspoken and unconscious agreements made within friendships.

As the following chapters show, such tensions and the unconscious agreements between women are now holding them back.

We are so accustomed to restricting ourselves and restricing one another that we have little practice with supporting ourselves and one another in the struggle towards differentiation. We barely believe it is possible and if it is then we conceive of it in concert. We all have to do it at the same time or else it is too threatening. We long to emulate women who manage to break free of the merged attachment but our fear turns into envy and we castigate them for stepping out of line and deserting us. We feel our inadequacy and can't imagine how other women are adequate and we turn our upset into competition and self hate. We feel guilty that we impede one another and furious at being impeded. We are angry because we long to stay in the merged attachment and we are angry because we wish to be separate. We project onto other women our fears, which are then mirrored back because other women have them too. We look for an all embracing, loving friendship or lover but we anticipate rejection and restriction. We have a deep and passionate attachment with one another which is at once holding and at the same time binding. In order to achieve more empathetic relating, in order to give and receive genuine support from one another, women need to move out of the constricting aspects of merged attachment into an attachment based on separateness.

Reference

1. Jean Baker Miller, in trying to rescue women's experience from the pathologizing of a patriarchal psychiatric establishment, has argued that, since women's identity is formed within the nexus of relationships, 'male' concepts of separation–individuation are not useful in describing the psychological development of women. Such concepts are superimposed upon a situation which they patently don't fit. In this Jean Baker Miller is undoubtedly right, for women experience their sense of identity in relationship. They know themselves in the context of the ebb and flow between themselves and others. But the problems with being so related to others and drawing one's self identity in this way has negative as well as positive consequences for women come to feel unclear about their own boundaries, their own selves. And it is some of the more negative consequences that are of concern to us in trying to understand the sources of some of the difficulties in women's relationships with each other. 'The Development of Women's Sense of Self' from the Work in Progress Series of the Stone Center for Developmental Services & Studies, 1984.

CHAPTER 4

Abandonment

Rena and Elizabeth are twenty-eight-year-old lab technicians in Edinburgh, who became friends through work three years ago. When they first met Rena was living with Adam. When Rena and Adam split up Rena felt depressed, lonely and bereft. Over lunch she would talk to Elizabeth about the things she was going through, her unfinished anger towards Adam, her fears of being alone, her doubts about ever finding another man. Elizabeth was single herself and had gone through several separations from intimate relationships, so she was able to lend a sympathetic ear. She knew the kinds of things that Rena was feeling and could sympathize easily. The two women began to spend more and more time together, going to movies, out to dinner, shopping, and generally developing a close companionship. They phoned each other in the evenings to chat, saying that they would see one another the next day at work.

Generally, marriages and sexual relationships provide the kind of relationship that Rena and Elizabeth developed. We know and accept that couples are dependent upon one another in all kinds of ways. But, even though we know that close women friends are emotionally dependent upon one another, we rarely acknowledge how important these ties are. When women are not involved in couple relationships, when they live alone or perhaps are raising children on their own, intimacy with a girlfriend may be their most significant adult emotional tie. It is estimated that 60% of women in their thirties are single. Like Rena and Elizabeth, single women friends speak to each other daily, go to social events together, plan their vacation together. In our culture, friendship is all too often allocated a secondary position, while only marriages and sexual relationships are seen as truly significant. However, this is in contrast to the experience of many women whose friendships function – for long periods of time – as primary relationships. When one of the women then becomes involved in a sexual or romantic relationship the abandonment the other may feel can be very painful.

For weeks Rena was attracted to a new biochemist at work. She and Elizabeth giggled over it at lunch and plotted strategies for Rena to meet him. For the most part Elizabeth was not disturbed by these conversations because their various interests in different people had always been a part of their friendship. But when Rena phoned Elizabeth up and excitedly announced she had done it, that she had gone up to John and introduced herself, Elizabeth felt a pang of upset. She listened to every detail of the encounter, asking questions and sharing in her friend's delight. But when she hung up she burst into tears. She felt a terrible loss and she felt frightened. She tried to calm herself by telling herself she was silly, that this degree of upset made no sense, but she could not rid herself of these feelings.

Because women derive so much of their identity and sense of well-being through attachment, and because women's friendships contain a merged attachment, a friend with whom one has made a significant attachment serves almost as a part of the self. The sharing of time, activities, aspirations, pleasures and pains transforms an individual sense of inner emptiness into one of rootedness and connectedness. When there is a shift in a friendship which involves or presages loss, two disturbing things can occur simultaneously. On the one hand a woman may feel somewhat disorientated, she may feel unconnected and at sea, as though she has lost part of herself. On the other hand, because the underlying emotional connection in female friendships resonates with aspects of the mother–daughter relationship, the loss or shift can stir up, consciously or unconsciously, the pain and anger women can feel about disappointing aspects of their relationship with their mothers.

Woman to woman relationships duplicate aspects of the mother–daughter relationship, as well as holding out the promise to each of the friends involved that it will repair some of the hurt and difficulties that reside in that relationship. Consequently in adult female friendships we can observe how frequently one or both members in a friendship have an unconscious wish to merge with the other person, to be 'mothered' and cared for, to receive the nurturing that they continue to crave. Each woman may unconsciously look to the other to make up for elements she didn't receive from her mother; she may feel dependent on her friend for support and encouragement and approval and, because she may need this so very badly, she may be in acute pain when her friend becomes involved in another close relationship. She experiences both the actual loss (of certain aspects of her relationship with her friend) and the feelings it triggers, about losing that intimacy and closeness she once had (or had longed to have) with her mother. The pain that is evoked may confuse her, for she may well be unaware of her continuing search and need for a merged attachment with her women friends.

Rena and Elizabeth's friendship did go through a profound change. When Rena started dating John she became absorbed in the excitement that a new love affair inevitably produces. Although Rena and Elizabeth still continued to see one another everyday at work and still had lunch together on most weekdays, Rena was less available. Her weekends were now almost entirely devoted to John and, although she made obvious efforts to be sensitive to Elizabeth, to be sure that they continued to make dates with one another, nonetheless the amount of time spent together had changed dramatically.

Elizabeth could not escape the deeply painful feelings of abandonment. The abandonment functioned on two levels. On one was the real loss of time spent with Rena. Weekends became difficult. She made what often felt like desperate efforts to spend time with her other friends, but many Saturday nights she sat alone in front of the television. But it wasn't simply loneliness that Elizabeth was experiencing. She felt depressed, hopeless and disconnected. Even those times when she went out with John and Rena, she was unhappy. She felt somewhat awkward, pathetic and out of place. Even when she was having a good time with them, enjoying a film or a meal, she couldn't be rid of the feelings of yearning for an attachment. No longer so central to Rena's life, Elizabeth felt cut loose. In feeling de-tached it seemed she had lost a part of herself. As Rena's availability diminished, Elizabeth became acutely aware of the emotional dependency she felt in their relationship. She now had no one to rely on for emotional intimacy.

Whereas everyone commiserates with a woman who loses a boyfriend or a man who loses his partner, and sees the loneliness that is part of a break up, few people take account of the loneliness and discomfort a woman feels when her relationship with a close girlfriend changes. Nobody rushes round with hot dinners or evening entertainments, and it would strike us all as very odd if they did. But the dependency girlfriends develop towards one another is not trivial and does need acknowledging.

The loss of a girlfriend through geography or through a change in her personal circumstances is significant. It does hurt. It does shake each woman up inside. It can feel every bit as severe an emotional wallop as a serious shift in a sexual relationship. It can render one temporarily fragile in similar ways. For all these reasons we need to pay attention to it, to recognize that changes and losses in significant relationships with women involve emotional retuning. Paying attention to the real adjustments that have to be made and the loss that is felt, is an important first step. If such adjustments can occur, then a space may be cleared for the complexity of identity issues – which may have become scrambled up in the merged attachment – to surface and be sorted through.

Elizabeth needed to give up on her feeling that she shouldn't be upset, for she *was* upset and she needed to accept it. If, together, Elizabeth and Rena could have acknowledged the significance of Rena's love affair for the friendship, Elizabeth might have felt less alone in her grief. She would still have had to bear the loss of the special intimacy on her own, but the emotional gutting she experienced, the feeling of being de-tached, would have been mitigated by Rena's support and understanding.

In providing this kind of emotional support, Rena would have had to be able to acknowledge and then override any guilt feelings she had about being in a sexual relationship. It may seem strange that 'getting something for oneself' engenders guilt but in her instance, and so many others we encounter, this *is* what occurs. Rena was subconsciously feeling that she had abandoned Elizabeth and part of her felt deeply guilty for having done so. She couldn't bear to see Elizabeth's pain, because she felt she had caused it by betraying her. Her guilt feelings then interfered with her ability to stay emotionally connected (on a new basis) and in touch with Elizabeth's needs.

The struggle that both women faced was how not to feel guilty towards one another or withdraw from the friendship. It was true that the equilibrium was broken, but that did not mean they couldn't find a new basis from which to connect and support one another.

The line between a genuine abandonment and an imagined one can be irrelevant in terms of the strength of feeling it stirs up. Because women's need of one another is so strong, although there is a taboo against openly

66

accepting this dependency, our antennae are alert to the potential presence of abandonment in a wide variety of situations.

Margot and Adeline are social workers and best friends. They've known each other since college and have been through marriages, children being born, postgraduate studies and career development, side by side. At forty-two, after her second child started kindergarten, Margot decided to enroll in an analytic institute which would enable her to become a psychotherapist. Adeline told her how wonderful she thought that was and how brave Margot was for trying it. Each time they spoke Adeline made a point of asking Margot where her application was in the acceptance process and was very supportive of her best friend. But, alongside her genuinely felt interest and support, Adeline was upset. She was worried that Margot's move to a new professional level would take Margot away from her. She hated herself for feeling shaky and upset and thought it meant that she was truly a selfish person and a despicable friend. She tried to reassure herself that this change needn't disrupt their friendship. Adeline reminded herself that she chose to remain doing case work and not to take on psychotherapy. Just because Margot wished to do something different didn't mean that what she, Adeline, was doing was useless or less valuable than Margot's work. But she was stunned to realize the strength of feelings she had. Margot's proposed professional advancement stirred up in her the same kind of feelings she had experienced when her daughter marched off to kindergarten and Adeline had sat in the car and cried.

The uncomfortable feelings that Adeline was aware of in herself are extremely common today. Her best friend's efforts to develop made her feel she was being abandoned. Her upset illustrates the ways in which the merged attachment, so often a feature of women's friendships glues a woman's sense of self together. When that merger is broken, the adhesive dissolves and the woman feels shaken up inside. She questions her own life to see if it holds up, if it is enough. Adeline had felt perfectly satisfied with her own work, but now that Margot chose to leave and move on to something new, Adeline felt as if she was left with nothing.

Margot, in her turn, had a complimentary set of difficult feelings to deal with. Margot was anxious about how to tell Adeline of her decision to do further training. She feared that somehow this news would upset her. Thus, when she did tell her, she did so almost apologetically, providing her with a long list of reasons why she may as well do this at this stage in her life. In the telling of this personal development to her best friend, she belittled the meaning of the act. Unconsciously she felt that if she made it less than it was, if she made it less desirable, if she made it appear to be less than what it really meant to her, it would not threaten or upset Adeline.

Both Margot and Adeline are women who have grown up to believe that other women will feel threatened by their self-development. While this is never taught explicitly, every woman is aware of the potential she has to arouse feelings of abandonment or betrayal in others, when she lets it be known that she is acting autonomously. A sense of danger and impermissability often pervades such acts on the part of women. Not only is a woman aware of the ways in which her activities and desires can cause pain to others, she may also be in some stress about acting on such personal desires, believing there is something wrong with her for wanting to take initiatives.

Understandably then, women have enormous difficulty approaching these things in a straightforward manner. While both Margot and Adeline were social workers, part of the security in their attachment was based on a commonality, a sameness. This allowed them to rely on their connection without question. In their connection they had given each other so much. It meant a lot to both of them. In fact, it was partly through the love and support that Margot had experienced in the relationship, that she had come to a more expansive view of herself. This now included feeling entitled to pursue a new career direction. But this very love and caring that flowed between them, on which Margot flourished, meant that there would inevitably be adjustments in their relationship. Margot's career change signified psychological differentiation: a break in the merged attachment.

Adeline worried that there might be a threat to the relationship, that Margot would develop new interests which she couldn't share, that perhaps Margot would meet another woman friend with whom she would share a new common experience. She couldn't securely hold onto the real attachment that she and Margot had. Breaking the merged attachment, which was an aspect of their relationship, made her uneasy. She felt abandoned. Consciously she knew that their friendship would survive the change, but unconsciously she feared their love and caring could not survive their separation. Margot, meanwhile, felt as though she was doing something that was somehow forbidden. She couldn't rid herself of the feeling that she was betraying her friend. She feared she would lose Adeline's support unless she stayed merged with her. In Chapter 8 we look at how Adeline and Margot talked about their fears with one another and the ways they were able to support each other in breaking their merged attachment, while still staying close and connected.

Christine and Andrea are best friends. They are both single and in their thirties. Christine is a kindergarden teacher and Andrea is studying law. They phone each other every night to check in and commiserate about the day's tiring events and they spend most of their weekends together. A strong theme in their relationship is the support they give one another around the dissatisfactions in their lives. Usually one or the other is in a bad state, upset or in a rage about something that has happened to her at work or in another relationship. Each wholeheartedly engages in the trials and tribulations of the other and offers unconditional support to her friend's position. It is as if they are on a see-saw, on which first one is up and the other down and then vice versa.

Christine and Andrea have a system worked out between them. They are locked in rage together and, although each apparently supports the other, the support simultaneously conceals a process in which they help one another cover up the tremendous pain each feels alongside the rage. As one jumps to the other's defence she is unconsciously identifying with the pain, the hurt, the deprivation. But, for each of them, anger serves as a protection against the deeper pain. They link arms through their anger and, as they commiserate, their joint anger creates a barricade against these painful feelings. Through their identification with each other, and because they share a difficulty in exposing need or hurt directly, their merged attachment served to keep their vulnerability hidden.

During Andrea's last year at university she met and became friendly with Julie. Julie was a self confident, contented woman who liked to enjoy herself. Andrea was drawn to her. At this point, having nearly completed her degree, Andrea herself felt a growing confidence and an optimism about life that was new to her. Whenever she went out with Julie she enjoyed herself. They went to shows, movies, dinners and always had a good time together.

Meanwhile, Andrea began to feel irritated with Christine. She felt annoyed with Christine's never ending sagas of mistreatment and victimization. The more aware Andrea became of Christine's negativity, the less she could tolerate it. Gradually she distanced herself more and more, until she had completely altered what had previously been a close friendship.

Christine, on the other hand, felt devastated. She was on an emotional rollercoaster. At first she felt jealous of Julie. She found herself saying critical things to Andrea about Julie and was aware that she was competing for Andrea's affection. She felt desperate that her efforts to win Andrea's care didn't work. What had happened? Andrea always supported and gave attention to her problems, why was she abandoning her now? Each time she spoke to Andrea and let her know how depressed she was, Andrea seemed to move further and further away. Christine was consumed with envy over the good times that Andrea was having with Julie and felt painfully abandoned and alone.

Christine and Andrea's attachment was built on similarities and resentments. When Andrea began to feel differently in herself, and liked the feelings of having and wanting more, the friendship shattered. They did not know how to change together or how to tolerate the differences that were emerging between them. They didn't know how to talk about the kinds of emotions they were having. Andrea felt she was betraying Christine when she told her that she was having a good time. Christine felt abandoned by Andrea. The difficulty these two women had in discussing their feelings with one another escalated the tensions. A gulf grew between them composed of both the difference and the inability to talk about what was happening. Andrea felt guilty and intimidated. Christine was hurt and furious. As in so many circumstances where differences between women friends cannot be aired or accepted, the situation between them became intolerable. The only resolution was a severing of the ties. Andrea was left with her guilt and Christine felt bereft.

The kinds of feelings that Christine, Andrea, Rena, Elizabeth, Margot and Adeline experienced, *vis-à-vis* one another, are often exacerbated in a group situation. This makes it even harder to understand the root causes of discomfort and dissension within groups.

When Laurie, the thirty-year-old founder and director of a women's dance company from Southern California took pregnancy leave the other company members felt abandoned. They went through a painful process trying to come to terms with the fact of Laurie's absence for a year. At first they were extremely nervous about forth-

71

coming performances. They felt incapable of putting it all together. They felt angry about being left. After the first couple of months, as they began to realise they really did have to take responsibility for running the company and could do so, a kind of disparaging contempt for Laurie set in. Their insecurity about running the company was suppressed, their former admiration for Laurie's capabilities was receding and there was a general denial of the early achievements of the company.

The emotional drama that unfolded becomes understandable when we remember that women's relationships with one another are loaded with a psychological significance quite outside the apparently straightforward professional responsibilities they share. We shall explore some of these themes in subsequent chapters, but for now it is important to see how the feelings of abandonment created havoc in the dance company.

The group as a whole related to Laurie as though she was the mother who would and should take care of them, never leave them, provide support and encouragement and a happy environment for them to work in. In transferring these hopes to the director, the group members psychologically gave up some of their own capacity to fend for themselves. There was a conflict between acknowledging their own competence and their continuing needs. Like many adult women today, the desire to be cared for was very strong. At the same time they all felt somewhat ashamed of such wishes, so they were never discussed or openly acknowledged. Although the group was composed of independently minded, competent and talented women, their outward confidence and high level of professional skill sat side by side with the vulnerable and shaky emotions each woman also experienced.

They responded in this way for all the reasons already discussed, about why women today are inclined to feel unsure and fraudulent. If anything, their dance training had compounded those feelings since it did not address the social and psychological pressures that women experience as they struggle to gain recognition in a profession. This was particularly true for dancers who were always expected to push themselves to be ever better. There was little sense of having achieved a position of being good enough, adequate, sufficient. Maintaining their status as professional dancers was itself a pressure. They were always vulnerable and were expected to be utterly dedicated, to be perfect at what they did. There was a disjuncture between their professional and private personas. Professionally they were seen as extremely confident and mature, while privately they each had feelings of insecurity.

Laurie's presence as director had provided each woman with a kind of antidote or safety net against confusing internal feelings. She had been seen as – and to a certain extent acted as – a parent who had given birth to the group and enabled it to function well. She was confident enough for all of them.

When Laurie was due to return to work after her year's absence, the group felt discomfort rather than excitement. There was a fear of reintegrating her. The psychological shifts the group had experienced in response to being abandoned now stood in the way of letting Laurie back in. This new consolidation of the group, that had come about due to Laurie's pregnancy leave, now depended on her exclusion. In other words, the havoc and upset caused by Laurie's departure had been managed largely by the remaining members bonding together. Of course, this was one of the few options open to them. Because they had felt so insecure and worried about her leaving, the group needed to find a new basis of support and connection with one another. They could bond together in the shared experience of abandonment and the survival of that abandonment. This new merged attachment provided them with some strength and a psychological basis for continuing. Letting Laurie back in, letting themselves once again feel her importance, would reopen the pain of the loss. In this case, it was not merely the loss of Laurie for one year but, rather, that the loss touched on much deeper feelings of dependency, attachment and need, for each of the women in the group.

The group had found a solution that sidestepped their feelings of dependency on and attachment to Laurie. In developing a strategy that kept her 'out'; they denied to themselves their need for her leadership and emotional support. When she returned there was an uncomfortable period of realignment. Some members yearned for the group to return to the way it was, while others were hostile to Laurie and criticized her new choreographic arrangements in an unhelpful manner. While these were very different responses, both related to the merged attachment that still existed in the group. Those who wanted to nestle cosily back sought a return to the original merger coalesced by her. Those who were fractious, were expressing how deserted they had felt when she went away. Her pregnancy had ruptured the merger and that was felt by some members, unconsciously, as an attack.

The group was not functioning well and tension permeated work. The company needed to talk about the psychological dimension of Laurie's pregnancy leave and her return. By bringing such issues into the open life of the dance company, less destructive responses could emerge. If the group could have found a way to *talk together about*, rather than enacting, their negative and insecure feelings, the dance company as a whole could have found a new basis for being together. Without necessarily understanding all the deep psychological meanings and ramifications, hearing one another's reactions to the new situation, and expressing their own, would have established a different way of relating. They would have upset the merged attachment and recreated a supportive work atmosphere on different terms.

It is possible to look at the difficulties women friends and colleagues have with one another as simply related to changed circumstances. Of course, as our circumstances develop and alter, it may well be that our friends no longer suit us or provide us with the stimulation, pleasure or support that we need. The friends we have in secondary school may be different from those we seek out at university or in later life. When we change jobs, or move from being single to being a couple, or *vice versa*, we may notice that, as our interests vary, so do our friends. For many of us, moving on to new things and saying goodbye to old friends is positive, especially where we have felt trapped in relationships that are unbalanced, draining or only dutiful. It is inevitable that new ventures and growth will mean new alliances and the loss of some old ones. Indeed some might argue that the upsets that Christine, Andrea, Rena, Elizabeth, Margot and Adeline felt are just experiences they should have been able to take in their stride. We can't count on things to stay the same in life, some might say, indeed, we would not want them to, and with change come hurdles that just have to be overcome.

But to take this view would be to both underestimate the dependency that exists in women's relationships and to denigrate their heartfelt experiences. Of course these hurdles have to be faced and overcome. There are friends whom we need to relinquish, and often we have to overcome some guilt in doing so. We feel guilt or sadness when we lose a friendship precisely because most friendships are very important to us at the time. They are neither trivial nor stopgap relationships. But, when it becomes clear that our interests have become irreconcilable and one has to say goodbye to a friendship, we often don't know how to do it. We don't have the conventions which apply to separations or endings of love affairs. We can say about a love affair that it was important for the time, but it couldn't last. We can savour it and feel regret that it was limited. But no such language enters discussions on friendship. Either we tend to feel guilt that we have abandoned a friend or anger that we have been left.

Friendship is not something we pick up and use as a convenience. Friends are not irreplaceable and interchangeable, even if, as we have seen, some of the psychological dimensions, especially replays of the mother–daughter relationship, are transferred from relationship to relationship. Each friendship is unique. Just as a love relationship gives something to each lover, changes them, helps them grow and develop in particular ways, so do friendships between women have a deep effect.

Within these friendships women grow, help one another develop confidence, receive love and nurturing, understanding and compassion. Paradoxically, the things women give one another help them to move out of the position of merged attachment. Gaining a stronger self-identity provides a stepping stone for growth and individuation. But as we have seen with Adeline and Margot, Christine and Andrea and with the dance company, a friend's changing circumstances can feel like a desertion.

There is an ethos within women's relationships – prevalent in both those informed by feminism and those with no formal regard for it – an ethos about staying in the same place together, or moving forward together at the same time. In other words, there is a sense in which difference cannot be allowed. It is experienced as dangerous and threatening. It invokes feelings of abandonment.

To put it crudely. The unspoken bargain between women is that we must all stay the same. If we act on a want, if we differentiate, if we dare to be psychologically separate, we break ranks. We are disrupting the known: the merged attachment.

We fail to trust that attachment and closeness can continue from a different basis, for we have no knowledge of this. We are fearful that the identity and strength we gain from self-development will cut us off from our still needed connections with other women. The tension between the urge to stay merged and the urge to separate exists simultaneously in women's relationships. Every woman senses that there is a price to pay for self-actualization. It engenders feelings of guilt in oneself while it stirs up feelings of envy, competition and anger in other women.

Sometimes our friendships can be the repository of our old ways of being. They contain the knowledge of who we were then and who we are now, they provide us with a psychological continuity, just as a family provides us with a chronological continuity. Because our friendships can give so much and help us to change, we do not want to jettison them, simply because that change can bring in its turn difficulties. By facing the unconscious fears of abandonment, by allowing one another to grow separately and within the friendship, we build the basis for a new trust within women's relationships.

CHAPTER 5

Envy

Amy and Lynn are good friends. Amy has been living with Mike for four years and has a year old baby. Lynn was divorced two years ago and has recently started dating men again. The two women are very involved in each other's lives despite their different circumstances. Lynn tells Amy about her various dating pleasures and fiascos and Amy tells Lynn about the newest things the baby accomplished on any given day. One night they are invited to a party, to which Lynn brings her newest lover. Amy and Mike have been at the party a while when Lynn and Ron arrive. Amy notices that Lynn looks radiant, sexy and really happy. She watches as Lynn and Ron do a sensual dance. Amy's heart sinks. Suddenly she feels fat, she hates her dress, her hair, herself. She is painfully aware of how little she and Mike are connecting. She feels envious. She rebukes herself for these awful feelings in connection to her best friend.

The following Sunday, Lynn is visiting Amy. Mike, Amy, Lynn and little Rosa are sitting at the dining room table over a lovely brunch spread. Rosa is adorable and Mike and Amy are clearly bursting with delight and pride over their child. Lynn watches the scene and feels despairing. She's thirty-five, without a child and without a relationship that might produce a child. She feels a failure, she feels alone, she feels envy towards her best friend who seems to have it all worked out.

Among the most painful feelings women experience today are those of envy towards other women. They occur once and cause discomfort. They occur a second time and the woman tries to avoid or suppress them. They occur a third time and the woman feels persecuted by these unbearable feelings. As we have discussed, with the changes in women's role and women's expectations over the last decade, our awareness of these emotions is on the rise, disrupting even the best of female friendships.

Perhaps they are feelings experienced towards only one particular woman, perhaps they are evoked only in particular situations. Nonetheless, they cause tremendous discomfort and shame. Lynn and Amy would have given anything *not* to feel envious of each other. The emotions came upon each of them, leaving them feeling tinged, contaminated, sick. Each had a visceral reaction to the unwanted sentiments, as if their very bodies had been taken over by foreign matter. Envy hurts, it can make one feel distrustful, it can stir up gruesome fantasies of revenge, it can create distance from a close friend.

Because there is no systematic or recognized outlet for such negative feelings in women's friendships when aroused they often find a psychological niche in self-criticism. Amy felt ugly and asexual, Lynn felt a failure. Each took the unacceptable and distressing emotion and turned it against herself. Having a negative response to a woman friend is so threatening that we feel safer in the pain of our own self-hatred. The woman feels hurt, pushed out, or angry, and assumes it is she who is at fault or lacking. She endeavours to repair her behaviour, or her character, so that the unpleasantness she experiences will not occur again. When these upsetting emotions rebound upon us forcefully and insistently, we may wish to deflect them. We may be so unused to experiencing them directly that we become nervous and anxious. We are more inclined to cover them up or turn them into something else. They eat us up inside, making us feel we are lacking. They cause us tremendous emotional discomfort and pain.

While Amy and Lynn didn't have a simple solution to their discomfort, they could have shared their pain and upset rather than turning it into self-denigration. Lynn might have told Amy how gorgeous she looked and complained about how frumpy she'd been feeling lately. In this way she would have been able to respond to the part of her that appreciated, rather than was threatened by, Amy's radiance and, in recognizing her attraction to what Amy had been projecting that night at the party, she would have seen that she wanted some of that radiance herself.

Lyn managed to tell Amy how dowdy she'd been feeling, Amy was immediately sympathetic and suggested they go on a shopping trip together, sort through Lynn's wardrobe, go for a facial or to the new hairdresser she had just found. Amy showed understanding towards Lynn's negative self-image and she was only too happy to help her change it. She'd been through such phases herself many times and knew how hard it was to get out of them. On one of their shopping expeditions, Lynn took the opportunity to say how lovely Rosa was and how sad she was not to have a family of her own. Most of the time she was distracted from such thoughts, especially when she was having a new love affair. But she knew Mike was not the kind of man with whom she wanted to have a baby and, when she spent time with Amy, she despaired of ever having such joy. Because the two friends could talk about the things the other had, that felt so lacking in their own lives, their longings didn't need to get stuck in envy, or worse, in self-disgust. Amy didn't deny Lynn's pain and upset. She responded in such a way that Lynn could cry and talk of her fear that she might never find a man she wanted to be with. Lynn felt better not always having to cover up the negative feelings she had about being single, or about her longings for a family.

While such conversations didn't do away with the pain either one of them was experiencing, they did remove the focus of the upset, from envy and self-hatred, into the area of their personal desire. Coping with those desires becomes a possibility, once the upset, which has been projected outward (onto someone else, with its concomittant distortions) is pulled back to its real focus. Lynn's sexiness and Amy's family life were things each desired. Instead of chastising themselves for these desires, they began to help one another accept them and fulfil them, in so far as that was possible.

As we have pointed out in Chapter 3, almost all women unconsciously transfer a version of the hopes and restrictions of their own mother–daughter relationship to their current relationships. Women relating to each other see, not just their friends or colleagues, but they project onto them a tableau of emotions which reflects the legacy of their relationships with their mothers. They want support for their autonomous development, but they expect disapproval. They want permission for their sexuality, but they fear punishment. They want to be cared for, but they fear they will be judged for having needs. Untangling the projections and the fantasies that fuel such feelings, is part of our current psychological struggle. One woman's success is often threatening to another. But why? The answer has been clearly expressed by hundreds of women we have worked with. They describe feeling deserted, left, abandoned, as the other woman moves on and develops. They feel as though 'the successful one' is turning her back, leaving her friend to stay stuck in the space they once shared. At the same time, the woman who is a 'success' feels alone in the new and unknown space. She may feel guilty about her achievements. Fearing that she is deserting the lot of women (her friend, her mother, her sister), she discounts what she has. She attempts to minimise it, to deny and hide her achievement. These dynamics, in which a woman feels guilty for her success and other women feel envy of it, were at work in a group of women psychologists in Chicago.

Hilary's work on child abuse was considered timely by the media and picked out by them for special attention. This catapulted the Psychology Research Centre, in which she worked, to national recognition. Hilary was asked to give interviews and speak on her topic all around the country. She became an accessible and visible authority and was able to make important statements about the nature of the problem and the treatment options that existed for victims and perpetrators.

While Hilary was extremely pleased to have the opportunity for the work and the Centre to gain such positive publicity, she found the exposure personally difficulty (Who, me?). The tightly knit group of six, which constituted the Centre's professional staff, began to feel like a group of five, from which she was somewhat excluded. She couldn't put her finger on anything explicit, but it felt to her as though she was now disliked and that they were critical of her. She began to feel uncomfortable around her colleagues and was aware of a great deal of tension in everyone.

During this time it was her husband, rather than her colleagues, who became her main support. He was impressed with her work and pleased for her that she was being given the opportunity to have the research widely understood.

When Hilary was first asked to comment on child abuse she had been extremely nervous. The staff had rallied round her, coaching her, trying to alleviate her anxiety and promising to stand by her. Now that she was clearly capable of doing such things, they found it hard to know how to relate to her. While they had known how to support her in her weakness, they were uncertain about how to support her in her strengths. To them it was as if, in becoming a spokesperson and managing that on her own, she had crossed a threshold. She didn't appear to need them in the same way any more. She had shown herself to be capable and confident and separate. They all envied and feared this in her. No one knew how to remain connected on this new basis and so they disconnected. In so doing, they cut off her anchor.

In disentangling the threads, Hilary was able to see that she had indeed contributed to her own isolation and the problems at the Centre. She had not been able to disclose how much pleasure she was getting from the public recognition. She was not able to share with her colleagues how her confidence had grown. She empathised with their nervousness towards the media and the public, but no longer felt exactly as they did. She found herself hiding her growth. She could not distinguish between telling a friend about some of the good things that were currently happening for her, and the feeling she was boasting. There was no way for her to share her good fortune, without the fear that she was provocatively stirring up envy.

Hilary's colleagues were, in fact, feeling uncomfortable about several things. On the one hand, they resented their Centre being solely identified with her work on child abuse, to the exclusion of other research interests. On the other hand, they were scared and envious of her growing stature and self-confidence. It was something they individually aspired to, but couldn't imagine achieving.

They were unable to examine their own envious feelings towards the success of their colleague. They found them disagreeable and, predictably, they had transformed them into something else – either private feelings of self-doubt and inadequacy, or rejecting and angry feelings towards Hilary. The tension increased to such a pitch that accusations began to fly around that she was competitive, self-serving and taking advantage of them. They felt they had all supported her but that, once she 'made it', she no longer needed them.

This change in a once mutually supportive relationship, points to the difficulties all the women at the Centre had in relation to Hilary's development towards separateness and autonomy. Hilary's experience might have been that of any of them if, instead of child abuse, the specialty of one of the others had been picked up by the media. The people, with these various feelings, would have been different, but the themes most likely would have been the same.

So much of women's relating revolves around supporting one another through difficult times. But, when a woman seems to be doing well, support may be less forthcoming and she may feel as though she is cast out of the company of women. Hilary herself had no desire to reject her colleagues or their intellectual and emotional companionship. She was as much in need of it as ever. She had begun to trust that her professional knowledge was sound, but she was still on fairly shaky ground emotionally. Criticism, withdrawal or rejecting remarks from her colleagues stoked up her *own* conflicts about ambition. *She felt guilty about her growth and isolated.*

The combination of an ambition to be seen and heard – that one is able to be part of a group and yet still be seen as a distinct individual, to feel confident and not hide one's strengths – coupled with an inability to feel that such desires are legitimate, form the mainspring for the kinds of problems in which Hilary and her colleagues found themselves enmeshed. Once Hilary was in the limelight, it raised the other womens' own desires for recognition; desires which they had not formerly conceived as being within their grasp and hence not in their consciousness. They envied the way she appeared to take the challenge in her stride and, instead of being able to feel proud and positive about their colleague, they felt inadequate, depressed and resentful. Her success brought them in contact with their own ambitions and longings; longings for recognition, for self-confidence, for an independent identity, that are still so new for women today. And yet, their own psychological barriers remained. *Tragically, as they held themselves back, they unconsciously felt driven to hold back another woman.* Her success, both public and private, symbolised differentiation and her differentiation stirred up too many conflicting feelings. It broke the known and binding merged

84

attachment which previously engulfed the Centre.

The mess of feelings that were tangled up in the situation began to loosen when Brenda, another researcher at the Centre, and Hilary initiated an honest talk about what was happening. As we shall see in Chapter 8, the impass was broken through conversations that were direct and honest.

Behind the feeling of envy lies, not the spoiling, ungenerous destructive person that is so much the woman's experience of herself when gripped by envy but rather, a person so deeply in conflict over her own wants and desires that she is frightened by the other's capacity to respond to hers. She admires the ability but can't understand how it is that the other can pursue what she herself feels so unable to pursue. She envies the other's capacity to give to herself in a way that feels deeply forbidden to her. She is stunned by another's capacity to fulfil herself. When we see another woman who, apparently, has fed herself we are in awe of her achievement. We may wish it for ourselves, but cannot imagine how we, too, could get there. When we see another woman groping towards self development, we may be so threatened unconsciously, that we try to discourage her. *In other words, what envy tells us about is the extent to which women are in conflict about their wants and desires. It tells us how women feel unentitled and undeserving. It is not so much that women are envious. Envy serves to immobilise us and in so doing it pinpoints our much deeper conflict about wanting.*

The emergence of envy can be seen, in this light, as a signpost to desire; a psychological defence, if you like, against women's wanting. It is not something to be suppressed as unsisterly, but an emotional response that we need to pay attention to. Defences develop to ward off, protect, conceal, distract, inner needs that the developing person fears cannot be met, or to cover something inside which a person feels unable to face.

The defence of envy allows one to project the feelings on to somebody else and so they become less internally disruptive and challenging. A partial solution is achieved with the idea that, if only a woman had what she was envious of, she would be alright. But, paradoxically, this solution feeds the feelings of powerlessness and leaves the woman feeling that her hands are tied. Rather than allowing for an active state of self-nurturing and development, she feels helpless, passive, needing to be rescued by an outside source.

The envy, then, shows us the craving, the strength of desire which is projected onto others. It is not a sign of unsisterliness, but a psychological reflection of the current conditions of femininity. If we are the object of envy we can understand another woman's envy of us as a sign that she hasn't given up; she still wants. We can help one another with these wantings, rather than stifle the feelings of envy as though they were indeed poisonous and destructive. In coming to grips with what is behind the envy, we create an opening in the merged attachment.

Envy is a contentious concept within psychoanalytic theory. Freud is well known for his early work on the concept of female penis envy and his finding that girls must overcome their envy (by converting it into the desire to reproduce) and accept their lack of a penis on their way to achieving womanhood. There has been many a caricature of a Freudian analyst wagging his finger over a female, insisting that she accept her inadequate biological/social status.

Melanie Klein, an influential figure in modern psychoanalysis saw envy as a feature of normal development. For Klein, envy occurs first in relation to the mother's breasts or the bottle. However adequate the mother is, Klein argues, the baby cannot control this real and symbolic source of goodness. The baby envies the mother's capacities, wants them for her own and wishes to deprive the mother of the richness that is in the 'feeding breast'. For Klein, each child comes into the world with a genetic endowment of envy (and aggression) which gets either softened or exacerbated by the environmental circumstances, such as the mother's capacity or difficulties in tolerating the baby's aggression. If these negative feelings in the baby can be tolerated by the mother, then the baby can pass through this phase to the next one, in which the capacity for remorse, and gratitude for what is being given, can be expressed.

Although both these views may seem radically different since in the original Freudian view it is the representative of the masculine that is envied, while in the Kleinian view it is the mother's breast and the feminine that is envied, there is, in fact, a great deal of similarity between both positions. Both Klein and Freud believe that envy is primary in itself and has to be faced as such. There is an inevitability about, a constitutional make-up relating to, the occurrence and persistence of envious feelings.

From our point of view, however, Freud's and Klein's observations bear reinterpreting. For the feeling of envy (while it can be extremely powerful in itself and can lead to destructive damaging impulses), can be better understood in relation to the struggles a child makes, out of the early stages of dependency and merged attachments, towards separation and selfhood. As we've seen, because of the merged attachment in the mother–daughter relationship, separation is especially problematic. When the child recognizes that it does not live within mother's boundaries, that mother is not an extension of it, it can feel frightened. Even though a mother's subjectivity may well be fused with that of her child, the mother's actions are not necessarily in tune with, or controllable by, the child. At various moments the child is forced to recognize mother's independence. The child may make many efforts to deny this, to control mother. And much frustration and rage is expressed when this effort fails. Both penis envy and envy of the breast can be understood as desires for what the child perceives the parent has (apparent self-containment and personal power). The envy is a question about having sufficient supplies oneself: "Do I have enough of what you have inside me?" "Am I safe enough to be my own person?".

Because simple examples of envy occur all the time and contain the same dynamics as the more convoluted and painful instances felt by Hilary and her colleagues in Chicago, let's look at two commonplace examples of how envy comes between women, and what can be done about it.

When twenty-eight year old Joyce tells her friend Rose that she has a new job as a senior buyer in the fashion department of Harrods, Rose, who is twenty-nine and apparently not ambitious, feels a twinge of envy. She remembers conversations they had at college when Joyce vowed not to settle for less than she thought she was worth. Rose had always marvelled at Joyce's aspirations. When they had worked in the same office, she had felt Joyce's support and the two of them had been promoted together. Two years ago, Joyce moved into retail and had already received several promotions and bonuses. Rose doesn't actually want Joyce's job, but she wants Joyce's self-confidence and the status, power and recognition that it gives her. Rose works in middle management for a wine producer and would like to rise but she can't imagine that she will be rewarded in this way and she has no expectation that she should be. She denies her own ambition to herself, but envies Joyce her promotion.

Jane and Monika are best friends. They met when they were both just out of university and working as very junior assistants in a publishing house. They were both energetic, thoughtful and likable and had climbed out of their junior positions to become senior editors for different publishing companies in their early thirties. Monika had her baby first and came back to work exhausted but exhilarated, just as Jane was about to have hers. The two women had lots in common, their work, their babies, their outlook on life. When Jane's baby was about ten months old, some of her energy returned. However, between baby, homelife, reading and editing manuscripts and keeping the other aspects of her job going, she had little time for herself and she felt dissatisfied with the way she looked and the way she felt in her body. Monika, it seemed, had acquired a whole new wardrobe, while Jane hadn't been looking, and she was trimmer and fitter than even before she had her daughter. Jane felt envious. She couldn't imagine how Monika found the time for herself. When Monika turned down lunch one day in favour of her exercise class, Jane felt mortified – a far stronger reaction than she might have though appropriate to a simple refusal of a lunch date. Jane's envy wouldn't dissipate. She raged inside about Monika's selfishness and then felt bad about envying her best friend. In talking to her husband about how angry she was with Monika, Jane realised that she wanted to make more of an effort to be 'selfish': i.e. 'for herself', in the way that Monika was for herself. In other words, she was able to use the discomfort of her envy to remind herself that she wanted some new items of clothing. She still dresses sloppily because her baby is dribbling and she doesn't want to ruin new clothes but, in fact, Jane is not happy dressing with baby in mind all the time. She wants more expressive clothes. Accepting her own wanting and since, in this case, the wanting is reasonably easy to satisfy, she can enjoy rather than envy Monika's new outfit.

In the first example, Rose cannot conceive of going after what she wants. She is lacking in self-confidence. Pursuing her own desires is outside her experience and her expectations. That does not mean that she isn't ambitious. She is. But this ambition is painful to her. It seems so out of reach. Her ambition is denied and her psychic energy is diverted to envying Joyce. Her envy, in effect, keeps her where she is. It prevents her from exploring her own ambition and the difficulties that surround it. The envy is an expression of her inner feelings of non-entitlement to advance or pursue her ambition. But it doesn't have to be like that. In the second example, we can see how, once Jane understood her envy as a signpost to her *own wanting*, she could get behind the initial discomfort that the envy provokes. When we contact our desire we can choose to act on it or not. We wrestle directly with the impediments, be they practical issues like Jane's baby still dribbling, or the conflicts which the wanting stirs up. We can try to come to grips with the internal voices that sabotage the pursuing of our desires.

For Rose and many women, the situations in which their envy is aroused cannot be resolved simply. As we have seen, women have come to identify the gratifying of their needs with the meeting of needs in others. Even though this is a far from satisfactory state of affairs, it *is* by and large what we have been brought up to expect and many women have accustomed themselves to a role and a self image in which they thrive on being needed. In the process of forging our new identities and finding out about the shortcomings of being so attuned to the needs of others, we are becoming more aware of our own needs – needs to initiate, needs for recognition, needs for support and so on. But women are doing so without a psychological feeling of well-being about putting their own needs on the agenda. They may believe wholeheartedly in women's rights or in personal rights; they may believe that whatever they want and in whatever direction their desires lie, they should make the effort to 'go for it'. But beliefs and feelings are not always confluent. Simply believing that self-expression ought to be allowed for women, does not necessarily make it alright. For example, many a woman has found herself sabotaging her own success. This is not conscious and certainly not intentional, yet we have to be able to take on board the uncomfortable and distressing phenomenon of women apparently undercutting themselves in their careers and in their relationships.

This is a hard phenomenon to confront for, on the face of it, it can sound as if one is 'blaming the victim'. But this is not our intent. We need to find an adequate understanding of a situation in which, for example, a young and extremely promising woman does badly in her PhD oral exam. Such a result cannot be explained simply by 'a wish to fail', but rather by a fear of the implications of success. Sandra wants to become a theoretical physicist; her mother gave up her scientific career when she married and Sandra's been determined that won't happen to her. All through university she worked hard. As a post-graduate she faced tremendous opposition to her choice of subject. People always assumed she was a technician, or teased her ambitions by calling her Madame Curie. No one was neutral about her participation in the course. She was never regarded in the same way as the male physicists who were supported, allowed to make the occasional mistake, and who were accepted for their work. She coped with discrimination and teasing and a certain level of social ostracisation. But one professor had been supportive and indicated several times his faith in her capabilities. So why is she 'giving up' now?

She appears to be crumbling at the moment of success because, as we discover in her therapy, success will confront her with a feeling that she is accomplished. Inside herself she doesn't feel entitled to that accomplishment. It does not feel real, she feels a fraud; it is so unfamiliar that in some sense she no longer 'knows' herself. She is more comfortable in the battle itself. She doesn't deserve it. She can only pursue her desire to be a physicist if it is fuelled by opposition. Her internal conflicts find a perfect expression in the attitudes of those around her, so she can rise above their opposition, even excel in the face of it. But getting her PhD would signify the end of the external opposition. She would then be left with experiencing directly her own conflicts and *internal* taboos pitted against her own ambition and belief in herself.

It became the task of the therapy to help her struggle through to the acknowledgement of her own wanting and to work through the internalised taboos against 'getting'. Accepting her success signified psychological separation and this was tremendously frightening for her. Although she had been determined not to repeat her mother's life, she felt a certain guilt as she crossed the threshold which would ensure she could stay in science. She knew it was what she wanted but a part of her felt uneasy. She was in unexplored and unknown territory. She was psychologically unaccustomed to the notion that she would be allowed to have what she wanted. Moving from a position of non-entitlement, of continual anger about not getting, to a position of achieving and succeeding, is an enormous psychological shift. It involves the transition from one kind of sense of self, to another. In the process there may well be confusing feelings of depersonalisation and loss.

For some women, the wanting that is behind the envy is felt to be unbearable. Sally felt envious towards Joy because of Joy's good marriage. Sally's husband had left her suddenly. Her ability to trust men had been severely damaged and she was forever warning Joy that she shouldn't rely so fully on her husband. Everytime Joy told her about a fight, disappointment or disturbance in her marriage (no matter how minor or commonplace), Sally leapt at the opportunity to remind her friend that she shouldn't expect more, that this is the way men are. For Sally, being the bearer of bad fortune and predictions was an expression of her envy for Joy's situation. She wanted to pierce Joy's idyllic picture, for the pleasure Joy was experiencing was very painful to witness. Beyond her envy, of course, lay her wanting for a warm and trusting relationship. She missed the closeness she had once had with her husband and she despaired about finding another man, especially now that she had a child. She would get in a rage about the situation from time to time and feel frustrated, alone and terribly stuck. The collapse of her marriage seemed to confirm for her the futility of the whole endeavour – her attempt at a close relationship with a man. Spoiling, or wishing to spoil, Joy's pleasure was an attempt to deny what Joy had and, in so doing, suppress her own wanting.

Envy then is a cue for an exploration of other feelings. Sally's envy was a defence against feelings which she found even *harder* to cope with. Sally's task is to approach the envy as a shield, which can now be removed to reveal the deeper personal issues. It is not simply envy in itself that Sally has to come to terms with – which of course she must also be able to do – but rather she needs to face her pain and the longing she has for an intimate relationship. One day, Joy became really annoyed with her for always latching on to any difficulties she had with Mike. Joy's rebuke bought Sally up short. She realised that damaging – in her mind – what Joy has, doesn't do what it is designed to do. It doesn't remove Sally's pain, it doesn't remove Sally's longing, it doesn't remove Sally's feelings of non-entitlement. It only makes Sally feel temporarily relieved of her own despair. In her disbelief and uncertainty about having what she wants, she does away with her friends contentment. She feels as though she can only tolerate her situation if no one else has anything.

This is a common phenomenon. The prohibitions against wanting are so strong in women, that it is very difficult to feel a genuine joy about something a friend has which we ourselves desperately want. Joy's annoyance helped to change a bad dynamic. Sally took it as an opportunity to think about why she was being so mean. The more Sally could accept and live in her current pain, the less she translated that pain and upset into the damaging responses associated with envy. She got closer in touch with her feelings of wanting and, agonising as they were, they did not impede her friendship or lead her to undermine her friend's pleasure.

A similar and nowadays extremely common situation took place in Linda and Joan's friendship. When Linda became pregnant at thirty-eight, Joan, who was forty and ambivalent about having children, tried to be enthusiastic for Linda's sake, but her personal turmoil got in the way. When they spoke on the telephone or went out together, they talked a lot about their mutual work interest in film, but Joan found herself dreading the time when the conversation would turn to babies and Linda's pregnancy. At those moments she felt so envious it was all she could do to stay in her seat. Hearing about the birth plans, or how Linda's breasts ached, or how much food Linda was eating, or how Mark and Linda were going to spend a last 'romantic' holiday for the two of them, almost made her wretch. She was literally sick with envy and could hardly concentrate on the conversation.

What perplexed Joan so much was that she wasn't aware of definitely wanting a baby herself. In fact it was almost the opposite. She was more aware of feeling she didn't want a baby and that made her uneasy. She had been in a stable relationship for several years and whenever the issue of whether to start a family would come up, she realised she didn't have a sufficiently positive desire to embark upon it. She liked her work as film editor very much. It involved a great deal of travelling and interesting challenges; she and Jonathan enjoyed their freedom and flexibility and although, from time to time, they could both feel a kind of existential angst that something was missing, for the most part they were quite content as a unit without a child. What made the situation difficult for Joan was that she didn't really believe, deep down, that it was alright for her not to have a baby while, at the same time, she felt scared of having a baby. She didn't think she would be a good mother and she couldn't see herself giving up her own interests and devoting herself to a baby. She was ashamed of these feelings and hated it when, in her dreams, they would force their way into her consciousness. Sometimes she would wake up in the middle of the night in a panic about being forty and childless. But in her conscious mind she didn't want a baby and couldn't really see herself with one.

Joan, like so many women today, is part of the first group of women who have had a choice about whether to mother. Contraception has brought incredible freedom and helped widen the options for women, but set against this is the fact that Joan, like other women of her generation, grew up believing that she would and should mother. The option not to mother is a recent

94

phenomenon, not something that was ever presented with equal validity. Consequently, Joan lives with a sense of discomfort. This discomfort is strong enough to prevent her from making a decision. She hasn't come to terms with not having a baby and yet she doesn't feel as though she wants one.

As Linda's pregnancy proceeded, Joan felt more and more insincere in her reactions and when the baby finally arrived, although Joan was happy for Linda and relieved that everything went well, she felt nauseous and anxious when she went to visit Linda. Joan was scared about picking up the baby, worried that she would drop it, or that it would start to cry. When she and Jonathan used to baby-sit, she would feel wretched. Jonathan suggested that perhaps she wanted a baby and that they should start trying, but Joan was alarmed at the idea and became cross with him whenever he brought it up. When Linda was raving on at her about how wonderful motherhood was, how Joan couldn't possibly imagine it and that she and Jonathan should really try it, Joan broke down and sobbed. Out of her tumbled forth her upset and distress and the confused feelings she had about herself, because she felt she didn't want to, and couldn't be, a mother.

As she cried with Linda, she was able to tell her that she had envied Linda's ability to know what she wanted. She wished she had Linda's forthright desire and wish to have a child. She wished she had felt that way, or at least felt clear enough and strong enough in herself to face the truth that she didn't want one. The issue of babies was a painful one, but her distress was compounded by her difficulty in making a decision. For years she had been able to push it away but, with her best friend's pregnancy, she found herself in an emotional whirlwind of envy, shame and fear. Talking with Linda eased her fears. The envy dissipated when she could see that she did need to confront these issues more squarely, for her envy represented her own longing to be resolved in this area. And could Linda tolerate it if Joan decided not to become a mother? Wasn't Linda's push for Joan to have a baby connected to a desire for them to be the same? Could she feel content with having something her friend chose not to have? Could they be different and still close?

These examples can, perhaps, put the concept of envy for women into a more understandable context. They underpin our assertion that envy is a signpost to wanting. In that light, as uncomfortable as these feelings may be, we can see them as rebellion and resistance to deprivation; as attempted declarations of desire; as psychological reflections of a competitive and divisive culture which has us believing in a theory of emotional scarcity – i.e. if one has, there isn't enough for the other to have as well.

We can feel guilty for our strivings and seek punishment for them. The unconscious equation that fulfilling oneself, succeeding in one's career, or achieving a personally satisfying love relationship, is a betrayal of another woman (mother) is extremely common. We can imagine, or project onto one another, disapproval and in this way we hold each other back. We can become threatened when a woman differentiates, when she deserts the image and practice of femininity in which we have all been raised. We can become frightened when a woman no longer acts like a victim. We can become both exhilarated and alarmed by a woman who displays internal strength, who refuses to pretend things are worse for her than they are, who seems to have overcome certain difficulties in her upbringing. Women's friendships today are under tremendous stress, performing a juggling act with a variety of difficult factors. On the one hand, women are making tremendous gains in their own professional and working lives, on the other hand, as we've seen, these gains produce emotional waves and reactions. Feelings of envy are increasingly familiar to all women. When such disturbances occur in groups, in organisations, between friends, then we face a challenge; the challenge of supporting one another, the challenge not to collapse under envy or guilt but to push forward to meet the longings that have been, up until now, only fantasies. In accepting our longings, we can begin to be active in relation to them, bearing in mind that there will be conflicts and uncertainties to face in this new and foreign emotional territory.

CHAPTER 6

Competition

Feelings of competitiveness often go hand in hand with women's feelings of envy. As in all the categories of emotional experience that women are reinvestigating and redefining for themselves, the phenomenon of competition, the emotions of competition, the concept of competition, raise many problematic issues. Competition among women has historically centred on winning men's attention. Women have competed with each other to have the prettiest dress, the newest hair style, the sweetest personality. The energy invested was considered reasonable and understandable in the days when women's lives were inevitably attached to men's. Women saw each other as rivals in a fight for men's attention and were often portrayed in movies and story book romances as endlessly resourceful in their attempts to beat a competitor.

However, when we look at this from today's perspective, with our realization of the importance of women's relationships with one another, it seems unlikely that the aim of such acts of competition, of making oneself attractive, or cultured, or 'nice', in one way or another, was simply directed towards getting men's attention. For many women, men provided the excuse, or the conscious reason, for making an effort with themselves, but the real target was just as often to gain women's attention. Women have sought each other's approval and competed amongst each other to obtain it.

From childhood on we have sought approval and recognition from women more than we have ever done from men. We have wanted our mother's attention and had to compete for it against other children, her family responsibilities, outside work, or her separate interests. For girls especially, the 'loss' of our mother's attention, which we have all experienced in the inconsistent nature of the mother–daughter relationship, and the encouragement to cope with that 'loss' by caring for others, often leaves girls feeling insecure. The turning to boys and men, while it replenishes some of the attention that we once needed so badly, does not replace the care and attention a woman may still yearn for from another woman. Nothing can. Throughout their lives women manage that loss in a variety of different ways. Sometimes they make very close friendships in which the wounds of the past, unarticulated and even unconscious, are healed by warm and nurturing contact; sometimes they manage the loss by appearing aloof as though they do not need; sometimes they choose girlfriends who let them down, thus reconfirming the original injury they experienced with their mother's turning away. For most women, a variety of responses are operating simultaneously so that, while a woman may have close friends with whom she is not in rivalry or actively competitive, a part of her may still be insecure with them. She wants to please them, in part because she likes them, and in part to ensure that she can hold their attention.

That is not to say that women are not rivals for men's attention. Of course they are and have been. A woman's social position, her visibility, the way she has been known (Mrs—) has, in the past, largely depended on that of a man's – first that of her father and later that of her husband. Thus competition to get the right man is a serious business. Its results have shaped many features of a woman's day-to-day existence. But the effort to

99

compete, the distrust of other women that it precipitates, finds some relief in women's friendship. In a sense, friendship was the best defence against rivalry for, in it, a woman could feel reasonably sure her friend would not compete with her for a man. Of course, occasionally women let each other down and broke the pact of friendship. Joanna's best friend 'stole her boyfriend and her job' leaving her in a state of shock; friendless, lover-less, and unemployed. Joanna and Caroline had met in Brussels where they were both working in public relations for international organisations. They had gravitated towards one another because they were both in their thirties, single, career minded and enjoyed each other's company. Together they would try and meet men and Joanna was overjoyed when she met Simon, a fellow Englishman working in Brussels for the EEC. Now they were often a threesome or a foursome if Caroline brought along a date. Joanna was very happy. She had everything she wanted. Caroline meanwhile was dissatisfied with the career prospects at her company and Joanna arranged for her to see her boss as that department was expanding. They fantasized about how much fun it would be to work together.

When Joanna returned from a two week business trip, her boss told her that he was so impressed with Caroline that he had hired her to oversee the department's expansion. Joanna was furious, she'd never expected such an outcome; neither had she been prepared for the affair Simon and Caroline had started while she was away. Although the two of them felt guilty about it, they worked themselves into a frame of mind wherein they assumed she would accept it and that their threesome would now become a sexual triangle. Joanna was incredibly distraught. She didn't want to, and didn't see why she should, accept sharing Simon. She felt she couldn't trust either of them again. She found it impossible working in the same office as Caroline and she left her job, although she wasn't immediately able to find another one.

100

Two years after this string of events Joanna told a workshop on women's relationships how much she still hurt, how she missed her friend and how angry and murderous she had felt towards her. She couldn't understand how these things had happened. To her, what was sacred in friendship was a sense of trust that those things which were important to one would not be derided or snatched away by the other. Almost everyone in the workshop nodded in recognition when Joanna expressed these sentiments, for women count on this bond between them.

When she had been a little girl growing up in the 1950s Joanna, like so many other little girls, had taken part in ceremonies, sometimes involving the exchange of blood pricked from little fingers, in which she and a friend pledged fidelity to each other. In those days fidelity was about keeping other girls out of the friendship or the clique, or sharing a particular hatred of a teacher or 'type' of girl. These confidences and the hating of others were as much building blocks in the friendship as the sharing of similar interests, ideas and dreams. Keeping others out and being able to put them down, 'to bitch' about them, was a safe mechanism for a girl's negative feelings (one of the few). But focussing on the dreadful outsider was really a mechanism for creating a safe place for the insiders. The need to feel attached and special to another girl is a longing which dominates other emotions. The competition which seems so apparent shields, to some extent, the more pressing and underlying need for safe, attached, love with a woman.

Competition is endemic to women's relationships. In truth, women have competed with each other in every arena. One moment girls and women are competing about who is the best dressed and, in the next moment, they are competing about who is the worst off in any given situation. "You haven't heard anything yet," says Sue, preparing to tell her divorce settlement story to a new acquaintance "You think you had it bad, well my ex-husband takes the cake." We swallow our guilt for

101

having been indulgent enough to think we were worse off and we listen diligently to the other person's story. We compete over how *well* we are doing and we compete over how *badly* we are doing. The competition disguises something else. That meaning is about a desperate need for attention; for someone to listen and to appreciate how it has been for us. We want the particulars of an event to be heard. We want our own private struggles to be authenticated by others and yet we can't imagine that they will be, unless we present them in dramatic ways. It isn't competition *per se* that shapes the presentation in this way. It is a sense that one won't be listened to – that one is invisible – that fuels the competition.

Kate is one of three daughters from a middle class family in Brisbane. Kate experiences a tremendous amount of competition with her sisters. She continually feels a strong need to distinguish herself from the others. In their own way, her parents tried to do this by praising different attributes in each of them. Linda was the 'bright' one who did well in school, Maggie was the outgoing one with a sparkling personality and Kate was seen as the beautiful one. But despite the parents efforts to give each one a special place, family and friends referred to them as 'the girls'. When, at thirty-two, Kate became the first of her sisters to become pregnant she gloried in the attention of her parents, her aunts her uncles and her friends. Three months later Maggie announced that she too was pregnant. Kate was beside herself with rage. She felt that Maggie had intentionally and wilfully taken something away from her. She found it almost impossible to show any happiness for her sister and dreaded spending any time with the whole family.

For three short months Kate had had what she always longed for – recognition and attention for herself from her parents; for three months she had the experience of stepping outside being 'one of the girls'; for three months she felt that she was being seen as uniquely herself, as Kate. Now she was filled again with the all too familiar feelings of competition. Once again, as 'one of the girls', she felt unrecognized and unseen as an individual. For Kate, competitive feelings were about her struggle to be seen in her separate identity.

The attempts that many women have recently been making to see other women as their allies, rather than as potential rivals, has meant that the feelings of competition may have been temporarily stifled, or managed in a slightly different way. But for most women they certainly haven't been eradicated by a dose of political insight or heart-felt slogans. In fact the situation today is perhaps even more difficult than it was a generation or two ago.

Today, as women struggle to take up their place in the world, to expand their vistas, to consider taking on and doing new things, they have a ready made masculine ideology being thrust upon them which goes roughly like this. The world out there is tough. If you want to succeed out there you also need to be tough. You need to know how to compete, to be single minded and firm. Competing is something men can and have done, it is bred into them, and women who want a slice of the cake will just have to take the pressure and compete in male terms. It's no good going all soft and feminine on the job. Competition is the name of the game in capitalist society. The strong survive and they do so by competing and by being on their toes all the time. In other words, women take note: you should be competing, for competition is a critical element of success.

It is ironic that much of the energy which initially propelled the Women's Liberation Movement, gathered strength from a consensus that competition among women was destructive; it divided women and made them distrust one another. Today, largely as a result of the campaigns organized by the feminist movement, women are now finding that more doors are open to them. But, instead of an infusion of feminine sensibilities accompanying women's entry, in significant numbers, into new types of jobs, we are witnessing the applauding of masculine values both at the workplace and at home.

Where, once, there were a few lone women in male jobs who were seen as aggressive or ballbreaking (i.e. not real women), now women at work are being encouraged to be as aggressive as men. Meanwhile, those women who fought it out for years on their own in male preserves, may have become completely accustomed to competing in male terms. As a result they are unsympathetic about taking up the challenge to consider work relations in a different way. Masculine values get strengthened as they are enacted by women[1].

The whole culture encourages and condones competition in one way or another. Competitive structures are embedded in our social relations. This is something which even those committed to social change for women applaud. Lillian Rubin, an American psychologist, in her lovely exposition on friendship[2] advocates that women become more skilled in dealing with their competitive feelings. "It isn't that the women don't have competitive feelings, only that they have much more difficulty in acknowledging them, therefore acting on them. Yet their inhibitions about competition can damage their friendships almost as much as men's facility with it harms theirs. Indeed, it is precisely because women have, for so long, been constrained from expressing their competitive strivings cleanly and clearly that they can become distorted into the kind of petty rivalries, jealousies and envy that sometimes infect their relationships with each other . . . As a psychotherapist, I believe one of my tasks is to help women to contact their competitive strivings more directly and to express them more openly . . ."

But this is too simple a prescription. In order to understand competition, what it means to women, and why they experience it in the way they do, we need to address some of the same sort of questions we asked when examining envy. For, as we shall see, masculine concepts do not serve us well in the analysis of competition.

Competition plays a different psychological role in the lives of men and women. Because of this we cannot import an essentially masculine concept without rethinking it. Just as envy, we argued, is a defence against a complex of other feelings, so too competition is a starting point in our understanding. Feelings of competition are disagreeable to experience, but they are not simply an emotional state of affairs that have to be grappled with (or applauded). Competitive feelings are a signpost to other feelings, a defence structure that, suppressed, clouds a relationship with difficult and unworkable tensions.

Let's look briefly at girls' and boys' psychological development, to see why the concept of competition has such a very different meaning for each gender. A crucial developmental task facing girls centers around being able to see themselves as *alike but separate* from their mothers. But, as we have seen, because of mothers and daughters shared gender, and because of a mother's identification with her daughter, and because a mother herself may not have a separated psychology (either from her mother or her daughter), this developmental process is not easy and many women are engaged in a lifelong struggle to establish a separate identity for themselves. Boys and men, however, are related to as 'other' from the beginning. They are unlike their mothers, they do not share their gender, they are fundamentally different, biologically, and they will have a different social existence from their mothers. And so boys are defined and have been defined in opposition to the feminine. They have a familiarity with otherness and difference. A boundary derived from gender difference affects the shape of the merged attachment in the mother–son relationship. Boys are treated as 'other' and experience themselves as 'other' from early on, and so the infant merger and the steps towards differentiation of self follow a different path[3]. Opposition is a stance that *upholds and supports* a masculine identity. Competition spurs the process of differentiation. It is an act of selfhood (albeit a defensive one). *Whereas women search for self through connection with others, men search for self through*

105

distinguishing themselves from others. Thus, competition for men is often about calling attention to difference, in the service of selfhood. For women differentiation can feel like a threat to self identity. It would, therefore, be a mistake to see competition between women as simply an expression of striving, and a skill they should be encouraged to adopt, or give vent to. We must first come to grips with what women describe as their difficulties with competitive feelings, and then explore those difficulties with reference to women's psychological history.

For so many women, the struggle for a separate identity is almost a psychic impossibility. Competing and differentiating feel equivalent to a severing of connection – a connection which has provided the woman with her sense of self. As we discussed in Chapter 3, the concept of differentiating, i.e. the capacity to be separate and still remain connected within the relationship, is outside women's psychological reference points[4]. To recapture the metaphor we used then, it is ungrammatical. It doesn't fit in with a woman's experience of herself or of other women. If one competes, one is in some sense contesting the merged attachment. The woman is saying I am not the same as you, I am different/better/worse. In forcing the separateness or difference to be acknowledged, she stands alone. And once alone or more precisely, unattached, a woman may be left experiencing a shaky self identity. Thus, competing can be an internally terrifying experience. For, in the act of competing, she may feel that she is threatening her relationship with the other. Competition does not hold them together but breaks them apart. She may feel as though she is annihilating the other woman, while at the same time losing herself.

As a result many women opt out of the competition altogether. It is no wonder women feel bad when they are competitive. It is no wonder they feel guilty when they are competitive towards a friend. It is no wonder that competition so alarms us that we often find it painful to admit to, or deny, that is what we are really feeling.

Presenting oneself as competent can feel too aggressive and self-serving. Finding oneself in a situation where one has to succeed over other women may be just too uncomfortable, because it is seen to sever women's lifeline to other women.

Marion dropped out of the Royal Academy of Dramatic Art (RADA) in London when she was nineteen because, although she was good, very good, she couldn't bear all the vying for attention that she and the other female students were involved with. She just wanted her talents and strengths to be recognised. She didn't want to have to be better than this friend or that one. She found it very threatening and was sure she had made the wrong career choice. She couldn't see herself competing with her contemporaries for parts, for the next forty years. She wanted a work situation in which she and others could feel intrinsically valued. Like many women, her need to find a self-identity in relation to others, rather than in opposition to, or competition with, them, precluded her from competing. It was simply too uncomfortable. Withdrawing was a more manageable stance for her.

Whenever Claudia, a musician in her mid twenties, was around Anne and Carol, two of her old friends from high school, who were now both professional dancers, she felt uneasy. With Anne she would suddenly start to feel diminished. With Carol she felt on edge. Even though the topic of conversation was usually one that interested her, she would rarely contribute to it. Whatever she considered mentioning seemed to revolve around her latest successes and she felt it would be too pushy to talk about herself. Claudia was an accomplished violinist and wasn't usually shy. She found the time spent with Anne or Carol very disagreeable and tried to understand why she clammed up. Eventually she came to realise that Anne and Carol were very competitive with her. They would talk about classical music never acknowledging her place within that field. They felt so bad about themselves and what they perceived as their lack of success,

107

that they begrudged hers. They tried to make themselves feel better at her expense. By disregarding her specialist knowledge, they effectively ignored Claudia and who she now was. It was this lack of recognition that raised competitive feelings in Claudia. She felt dismissed and almost banned from taking part in the conversation. It stimulated a strong desire to display her talents, to force Anne and Carol to acknowledge her, but she was so angry and hurt at being disregarded that she simply choked.

Often competition is about the desire for recognition of one kind or another, because outside recognition grants a person visibility. If one feels passed over, unseen or squashed, feelings of competition may erupt that represent a fight for selfhood. A woman wants her achievements to be noticed, for *her self* to be seen. Claudia wanted to force her presence on Carol and Anne. In being ignored by them, she became invisible. An internal alarm went off, making her fight for her place. Her wish to talk about her latest accomplishments was an effort to bring the recognition she had gained elsewhere, into a situation where she wasn't being recognised. Anne and Carol *were* in fact ignoring Claudia. Their envy stood in the way of their acknowledging her. Because Anne and Carol were each, individually, in conflict over their own longings, their own ambition, their desire for public recognition, they had to deny Claudia's achievements. They joined together excluding her and her contribution. *Their envy stirred up her competitiveness*. Their denial of her made her fight for herself.

Let us recall the psychologists in Chicago, to illustrate the interplay and differences between envy and competition. We discussed how envious Hilary's colleagues were of her budding self-confidence and her ability to grow into her new public role. What we did not bring into the story then was that, in addition to their envy, they felt competitive. For, as well as the repressed ambition that ignited their envy, they had competitive feelings about the recognition she had gained. They wanted equivalent recognition for themselves. They wanted an 'outside' acknowledgement of their competence. Inside themselves they did not always feel competent and adequate, but they wanted to. If they were in Hilary's shoes, they fantasized, they could gain the affirmation she had received, enabling them to feel competent too.

Whereas feelings of envy stem from a taboo against a woman's wanting, feelings of competition stem from the prohibitions they have experienced regarding their autonomy and visibility. Unlike envy, the woman feeling competitive is not trapped in conflicted impermissible longings. Rather, her struggle is that she feels undermined by inadequacy and self-doubt. She doesn't feel capable or competent. She doesn't know how to go about gaining these qualities. She is ashamed to expose her feelings of inadequacy. Admitting them is so humiliating and frightening that they become turned into their opposite: "I can do better than you." Even where the competition is about how badly things are going, it also contains this element. For, if things are very bad nothing can be done. One is hopeless. Competing about being the best or the worst are two different faces of a defence against facing deep feelings of inadequacy.

In the same way that we can understand aspects of envy as a rebellion against deprivation, so too can we understand the impulses behind competition in a positive light. Women's feelings of competition are an expression of their energy towards life, towards self-actualisation, towards differentiation and the right to be one's own person. They are about the desire for separation and selfhood. They are about overcoming crippling feelings of self-doubt and insecurity; they are about wanting to achieve the confidence to fulfil ambitions; they are about having and being.

To see them in this new light, however, is not to disregard how painful and humiliating feelings of competition can be. In unravelling the various threads, in investigating the competitive feelings, we are always asking why a woman feels competitive with another woman. What is at stake, what is the function of the competitive feeling?

If we bring to mind again the Southern California dance company that Laurie initiated, we may recall how upset the others felt when she first went on leave. They had to overcome feelings of abandonment and insecurity. When she was about to return to work, they found themselves wary about reintegrating her. Part of their unease was expressed as competition. To understand what was packed into the rubric of competition, this example shows us three distinct features which can occur between woman. (1) competition for outside recognition (Laurie had recognition as the founder and director), (2) competition as a cover for feelings of inadequacy and (3) competition in the search to assert a separate identity.

Several of the women revealed that they felt openly competitive with Laurie, her choreographic skills, her ideas and her flair. During the year she was on leave, without her to rely on, they had been forced to develop talents they didn't know they had. While they were nervous about doing so, they had performed two new dance sequences to acclaim. They had gathered for themselves some of the recognition she had previously received and they were loath to give it up.

Because this was a new direction for them as a group and because it followed closely the tremendous insecurity they had felt when she went on leave, her return was threatening. They worried that she would come back and dominate the group. They worried that she would come back and take away what they had accomplished. They worried that she would find their efforts pallid by comparison with her own. They feared that when she returned *they themselves*, not her, would deny the strength they had amassed and that they would be unrecognised by her, because they would hide what they were now capable of doing. Her absence had lasted long enough to uncover their own feelings of inadequacy, but not quite long enough to consolidate a new source of strength. They were insecure and wanted her approval. At the same time they couldn't imagine they would receive it.

When she had gone on leave, the group inherited a baby (the dance company) which it had never parented. They felt very competitive with Laurie in the sense that they wanted to be adequate parents, but they feared they were not. They worried that she would see that and feel disappointed in them.

Their dilemma involves many of the problems that hide behind the term competitive – feelings of inadequacy, lack of recognition and struggle for a new group identity.

Sara and Lesley, both journalists at a local radio station, are for ever going on diets together. After three weeks of the latest one, Sara tells Lesley that she has lost twelve pounds. She is terribly pleased with herself and expects Lesley's praise. Lesley instead feels competitive. She's only lost seven pounds and until she heard Sara's news she was feeling quite pleased with herself. Now she feels fat and useless. Sara's triumph doesn't inspire her, it makes her panic. Lesley feels deserted by Sara. They were supposed to be miserable together or successful together. They were meant to be in the same place at the same time. Now Sara has done something to break the bond. All of a sudden there is competition where there was none before. And in the competition, Lesley is losing. She wishes she could do as well as Sara. She feels competitive. She feels mean for being ungenerous towards Sara.

Lesley's competitive impulses were a simple example of competition functioning as a defence. Her merger with Sara allowed her to feel relatively secure and good about herself. She wasn't alone in her dissatisfaction about herself and she wasn't alone in seeking (albeit temporary) solutions. When she was doing well on her diet, she was able to feel relatively good in herself. But when Sara told of her success, she instantly experienced herself in relation to Sara. She felt the differences

111

between them. Her good feelings evaporated. Sara's success induced in Lesley a sense that she could never be good enough, attractive enough or sufficiently self-disciplined. She wanted to give up on her diet because she felt such a failure and a slob. These feelings had been kept at bay as long as the agreement to stay together in the same place was in force. When Sara 'pulled ahead' of Lesley, Lesley's competitive feelings made her want to pull ahead too, but her inner experience of inadequacy surfaced simultaneously stopping her in her tracks.

Of course it wasn't Sara's fault that Lesley felt this way. Lesley's upset was something she had to overcome in herself. Sara could help her with it, but she hadn't actually abandoned her by losing more weight. She hadn't been trying to compete with Lesley and do better, she had been trying to do what she wanted for herself. When they talked about how discouraged Lesley felt, Sara tried to renew Lesley's confidence, to help her overcome the feelings of inadequacy that Sara's relative success had aroused.

Is it inevitable for women to feel rivalry towards one another? Is this competition engendered by the mother–daughter relationship? Underlying each competitive situation, is there a fear of surpassing what mother has achieved, or perhaps a desire to surpass what the mother has achieved?

Of course, themes from the mother–daughter relationship resonate for most women when competitive feelings are evoked. In forging our identities we have had to compete with the overwhelming image of womanhood that mother's presence represents for us. We have needed to reposition ourselves vis-a-vis her. This may be a painful struggle for, in finding new options for oneself, it can feel as though one is rejecting or repudiating a mother's life and what she has given. In order to be a grown up woman oneself, one may feel that one is betraying or deserting one's mother, getting for oneself something she has never had – the experience of separated selfhood. If mother's identity is derived and maintained from her merged attachments, then a daughter's separation may be resisted. A mother may wish to keep her daughter in the merged attachment in order to maintain her own identity.

Mother and daughter may feel that they are engaged in a tug of war. At times, one is pulling for the merged attachment, and the other for differentiation and separateness. Each can find herself on either side of the rope, for they both desire merged attachment and they both desire separation. Neither can win, as long as they go on tugging, because this is not a war, but a joint and separate struggle for selfhood. The daughter's struggle towards adulthood may, therefore, feel full of competition, as though each circumstance is a test of who will win. Each one feels trapped in the struggle. One feels she has been abandoning and betraying, the other feels she is the prison guard. But this need not be a fight for individual survival based on either merger or false separation, if the love, connection and need which they have for each other, as well as the pain and joy of letting go, can be acknowledged.

One obvious area in which we can see the mother–daughter competition emerge is around a daughter's developing sexuality. A teenage daughter symbolises a mother's transition to a different stage of her life. And because our culture places a premium on youthful appearance and sexuality, it is not an unproblematic transition. Sexuality has been an asset a woman has taken into the world[5]. It is through her sexuality that she has been recognized, albeit only partially. Because of this, a mother may be fearing her own aging process at the same time as she is encountering, on a daily basis, her daughter's entry into the world of sexuality and womanhood. Her daughter's nubility reminds her of how her physicality was once an important vehicle for her to receive recognition. Thus without even being aware of it, a mother may struggle to maintain her 'self', by sexually competing with a daughter.

Many women have spoken about the ways in which

they felt their mothers became overly intrusive and involved with their boyfriends. Indeed this is such an accepted part of the culture that it was mythologized in the role Anne Bancroft played as Mrs Robinson in *The Graduate*. Mrs Robinson's power, such as it was, was essentially sexual. Her terror of aging, of not being seen as a sexually desirable person makes the emerging sexuality of her daughter too painful. She desperately clings on to her own sexual identity as she fights with her daughter for the limelight.

In the various struggles with competitive feelings which women are having to face, we can see a common thread, a common desire that can help us rehabilitate the notion of competition, rather than simply recoiling from competitive situations. Instead of feeling terror when we experience our own competitiveness, instead of being paralysed when we act competitively towards a friend, instead of judging ourselves negatively, we can look at competition as a way into understanding more about ourselves and other women. We can see that it is, in part, a search for recognition, an aspect of the struggle to self-actualize, to separate psychologically, to be seen wholly as an individual. It is not about defeating the other person, it is not about being 'the best', it is not about external accolades *per se*. It is about using the example of someone else's achievement, in whatever direction that might be, to try and fulfil one's own personal ambition.

Women's appreciation of other women's successes and achievements can pose problems, if we rely on patriarchal constructs to evaluate what is admirable and worthwhile. In our society, another's achievement is often experienced together with competitive feelings. Such responses are deeply embedded in our culture but – we argue – they are expressions of a system which promotes individualism, self-promotion, fear of intimate social connection.

Individualism is a reward system and a way of being that fosters false independence. It doesn't require the person to have a secure sense of self. One denies one's dependency on others and continually builds on a set of defences which isolate one from intimate connection with others. Others' achievements can be experienced as a threat, for one relies on a sense of self from outside of oneself. That is, lacking an internally secure sense of self, one builds a personality based on outward achievements. One is continually thrown back on competitive feelings, for one's very existence rests on external appearance and successes. Tragically our culture endorses and thrives on this latter formulation. The system we know of competition, dog eat dog, superstar and underdog, is built on individualism.

In contrast, psychological separateness, that is, the ability to feel a sense of oneself, and a boundary between self and other, is not the same thing as individualism. Psychological separateness encourages and makes possible fulfilling and authentic connections between people. The ability to achieve a sense of oneself as separate, derives from being in a connected relationship and acknowledging one's need for love, interdependence and emotional connection. This need carries on throughout life. Relying on others is a central part of psychological separateness. In building an alternative to destructive competitiveness, we need to pose a different structure to relationships: a structure which can contain both connection and separateness and the creativity that flows from that tension.

References

1. In her book, *Feminine Leadership or How to Succeed in Business Without Being One of the Boys*, (Times Books, 1985, New York), Marilyn Loden makes a strong case for the potential of creating new forms of feminine leadership that do not replicate the traditional masculine, competitive ones. She points out that throughout the 1970s, in business, there was a tremendous lack of worker interest and commitment. Psychologists called in as consultants to develop ways to deal with these problems

115

proposed a change, to a more personal mode. Loden argues that the more personal mode is a trend which complements femininization of the workplace, and that women's skills have more of a place in these newly developing mores. Not only will there be less of a split between what is feminine and what constitutes leadership, but women will be seen to have the essential skills which all successful managers must learn, thereby giving women their rightful recognition and respect. The current mandate that a woman adapt herself to fit in to a male mould may not be the only option.

2. Lilian Rubin, *Just Friends: The Role of Friendship in our Lives* (Harper & Row, New York, 1958), pp. 83 & 89.

3. See Eichenbaum & Orbach, *What Do Women Want?: Exploding the Myth of Dependency* (Michael Joseph, London, 1983). For a discussion of the developmental differences which lead to men's difficulty with connection and intimacy and women's difficulties with separation and intimacy.

4. See Eichenbaum & Orbach, *Understanding Women: a feminist Psychoanalytic Approach* (Penguin, London, 1983).

5. See Susie Orbach, *Fat is a Feminist Issue* (Arrow Books, London, 1978).
See Susie Orbach, *Hunger Strike: the Anorectic's Struggle as a metaphor for our age* (Faber & Faber, 1986).

CHAPTER 7

Anger

Anger is an emotional state that tends to present enormous difficulties for women. We have grown up with two entirely contradictory images about women and anger. On the one hand is the contented, mother figure who accommodates others and for whom nothing is too much. She is unflappable, absorbs everyone else's pain and upset and projects warmth and ease. Anger and angry feelings never surface in her. On the other hand is the angry, nagging shrew. She is dissatisfied with her lot and flies into a rage at the slightest provocation. It is disagreeable to be around her and her anger is portrayed as vicious and damaging.

These two caricatures of women deny anger a place in her emotional vocabulary. The message we are left with is clear. She is not supposed to feel it and, if she does, she is certainly not supposed to show it. As with their sexuality, women are represented in two extreme ways, saints or shrews (madonnas or whores) and, as with their sexuality, almost everyone – including the woman herself – is afraid of a woman's wrath. In women's relationships with one another anger is rarely acknowledged or expressed. Although difficulties, disagreements, inconsiderateness and so on, which provoke anger, are every bit as much a part of a friendship as they are part of other intimate relationships, women have no direct outlet for the anger such upsets may cause. While mothers and daughters may fight with one another, and sisters squabble incessantly, woman to woman relationships outside the family rarely include arguments about personal difficulties, and when a dispute does reach breaking point, it may well be that its tenor is loaded with guilt and accusations, making it intolerable for both parties concerned. Often a rage ensues that terrifies both women, discouraging them from showing their angry feelings towards one another again.

From the Introduction to this book you may recall that it was the ferocious anger which women expressed in the Women's Studies Programme at Richmond College in 1972/3, that led us into a deeper study of women's psychology and a desire to understand why women, who could unite in the face of opposition, became immediately adversarial when the external opposition faded into the background. By analysing now – at a psychological level – what took place in that Women's Studies Programme, it is possible to see that the disputes and difficulties which occurred, the political disagreements and differences of opinion that emerged, took on a psychological significance well beyond the scope of the original strictly political nature of the dispute. In a sense it was as though this dispute – and others similar to it – carried the weight of all the unexpressed difficulties and angers that do exist between women. When these difficulties erupt we are not witnessing a simple difference of opinion, but the expression of a very deep enmity that can be stirred up in women. When the love and trust they count on from each other is eroded, then the upset, betrayal, hatred and rage that is evident becomes extremely powerful.

At one level, we could say that what occurred in the Women's Studies Programme, what fuelled the anger and feelings of betrayal, guilt and rage, was a breaking of the merged attachment that had initially held the women in the Programme together. The members of the department had joined and created a feeling of security by focussing on their common experience vis-a-vis an outside 'enemy'. The difficulties and differences between women – which they are so unused to dealing with in a straightforward manner – could be subsumed as long as a forceful opposition existed outside. The opposition strengthened the resolve of the insiders, bound them together and was a useful dumping ground for the difficulties within the group. When the Programme had received the bit of support that allowed it to function, then the disagreements about its philosophy and direction emerged. But these differences were threatening, because they represented a challenge to the safety and surety of attachment based on merger and sameness.

What made the situation so explosive and ultimately so damaging was the way in which certain women could not tolerate difference. They could not hold onto the good feelings in the group and trust that their opinions would be valued, unless the whole group agreed with them. These women looked to the group – as a kind of transferred mother figure – to give them the approval, love and support that they still craved. In others words, the insecurity we have seen which leads friends to want one another to agree with them absolutely, or be in exactly the same place at the same time (Lesley and Sara), was exacerbated in this particular group. Their strongly held political views were felt by them to be invalidated – and by extension they were invalidated – unless they could control or dominate the situation. Any diversity was intolerable, for it could not sufficiently answer the psychological insecurity of the women who were bonding together politically in order to find that psychological security. It was as though unless their positions were the dominant or the only position, their *very selves* were in question. The search for identity and selfhood had devolved upon the group and when it refused to be a shoring up operation, the rage that was unleashed was tremendous and destructive.

At the same time, because they were insecure, not

used to being taken seriously, listened to, appreciated and so on, group members found it hard to believe that diversity of opinion was valued and that an opinion would carry weight even if it was not held by everyone. A women only environment had opened up the longing for just that kind of attentiveness but, along with the longing (conscious and unconscious) was the remembrance (conscious and unconscious) of what a woman (the group) could not give, of how a woman was restricting; in other words, the enabling–disabling nature of the mother–daughter relationship.

Psychologically, the group turned from being experienced as a good and nurturing mother who is enabling and helps one grow through the merged attachment, into a disabling venomous, withholding, mean traitor that must be destroyed. The group (the mother) could not psychologically provide for all the needs that were unconsciously being brought to it. Nor could it make up for what had been missing in each individual woman's past, and yet the unconscious wish that it could do so was very strong. When that unconscious fantasy broke down, the rupture was full of the rage of disappointment and the self-hatred that comes of believing that what was missing might have been there. Having allowed oneself to be seduced into hoping that the Programme might mend the hurt and anguish left over from the primary mother–daughter relationship, disappointment and humiliation are rife. The group has to be torn apart, the original unity repudiated, a premature separation instituted, because differences are so painful that they have to be denied and negated. Once again, in the group, the mother is found to be duplicitous; enabling and disabling.

The inability to cope with difference, which is at the heart of many of women's difficulties with one another, is a compelling force in women's anger. The anger plays a role in both the denial of differences and in the assertion of difference. In the Women's Studies Programme, it served to eliminate a difference that couldn't be handled.

120

The protagonists were caught up in a struggle in which anger and rage became the mechanism for the silencing of others and for the assertion of self. In this sense it had both destructive and constructive meaning. This happens in other situations too. Often a woman will feel herself becoming angry when her experience or perceptions are being denied. With the denial it is as though *she, her self*, has disappeared. Her anger emerges as an act of self-proclamation. She is asserting her right to be seen, contesting a view that says differences are untenable. And yet this self-assertion may be problematic, because it threatens her links with other women, with whom the need for attachment remains.

If we think back to the situation between the violinist Claudia and her friends Carol and Anne, we may recall that Claudia felt angry and competitive when she was excluded from the conversation. Her anger at being ignored produced in her two distinct responses. One was to clam up, further distancing herself from the conversation. The other was to respond by 'boasting' – trying to force her presence on them. The anger she felt, which stimulated both responses, contained both negative and positive aspects. On the one hand, it was an alarm bell signalling a fight for visibility in a situation where she was being denied recognition, on the other hand, it further immobilised her, making it extremely hard for her to contribute to the conversation in a way that felt comfortable.

For many women, anger is just as it was for Claudia. It is a signal that all is not alright, but at the same time the person doesn't quite know what to do with 'it'. It may take her over, she may feel shaky, depressed, weepy or out of control. She may misinterpret her angry feelings and not know what to do with them. Anger is so fundamentally out of place with the cultural stereotype of femininity that, even though we all feel it, observe it and have been the recipient of someone else's anger, we can be scared of it in ourselves.

Much of what is embedded in women's anger is

caused by a psychological misreading of a situation. As we have established, the transferences between women, in which they are seen as one another's mothers, can sometimes cause confusion about what they are needing, wanting and anticipating from each other. Often a woman will project onto a friend disapproval where it doesn't exist, reading in her facial expression or responses the condemnation of her mother. In turn she feels angry that she has been rejected. She feels she is not allowed to have whatever it is she wants and the anger is a way to bolster her sense of self. In expressing herself, or in hearing her anger, she feels stronger.

But, of course, not all angry feelings in women have as their root the tangle of projections and transference phenomena we have referred to. Women feel or become angry when an injustice has occurred; when they have been hurt, when they feel taken advantage of, when they feel misunderstood. The difficulty is that they are more than reluctant to display this anger to a friend who may have caused it. Similarly, the knowledge that someone is angry with her, may make her nervous and fearful. *It is at this point*, not in the recognition of the anger, but *in the anticipated delivery or receiving of it*, that the transference projections occur. When we were little and we aroused our mother's or father's anger, we felt afraid. The anger they directed at us felt like a withdrawal of love. In that moment, the world became a frightening place, for without the protection and love of a parent, we feel vulnerable and scared. Even if our parents were not all that we would have wished them to be, their withdrawal, synonymous with anger in many families, was a withdrawal we could ill afford, for we still needed them.

When we were little and we felt anger in ourselves, we were also frightened. How dare we feel angry at those we still needed so much. To feel anger and especially to express it, would be to jeopardise the relationship. We would be cutting ourselves off from the source of comfort and succour. It is easy to observe how anger is related to the development of an individuated self. Observing

122

two-year-olds one can see that it is not that they are 'terrible' as in the cultural adage, but that they are in the process of differentiating, expressing their differences, asserting their will. When their way is interrupted, when someone else misunderstands what they want, they assert themselves with vigour. The act of assertion, if accepted by the adults, allows them to feel safe in their identity and desires; their anger is understood and tolerated. If the act is continually thwarted they will get in a rage as a way to preserve a sense of self. The tantrum that follows is an assertion of self, an attempt to protect and insist on their still fragile and developing, separate identity.

Another aspect of anger occurs for those women who grew up in families in which angry feelings were forever being expressed, and where violence was part of the family's way of relating. In such cases anger becomes associated with the capacity to arouse strong emotions. It is a known form of contact. It shows that the other person cares. While not a version of love, it is an expression of the intensity of feeling. It may signify love to one who has not felt the nurturing, supportive love of a mother or father. Rousing someone to rage, engaging with them in an angry manner, gives them some feeling of power, even if it is only a negative power. At the same time, in the combat there is contact and a common experience – albeit a very painful contact.

With this background, anger between women is a fraught arena. It touches on the anger of early childhood and threatens the established relationship. But it is not the whole story, for if the anger can be spoken of without the person feeling they are out of control or damaging the other, it can be useful to both friends. To express one's anger is to hear oneself, to defend oneself when one had felt invaded, negated or denied. If Claudia could have expressed her anger directly to Anne and Carol, 'I feel angry with the two of you, I don't like being ignored. I want to be included and recognised,' she would have found a more authentic expression of her feelings than

123

the boasting which caused her such discomfort. In that act of assertion she would be saying, 'See I have a self, I'm human, I hurt, I want. I am not just a trash can into which you deposit your difficulties.' Carole and Anne would, in turn, have to deal with real criticism and cope with the hurt they were causing. This might have helped them understand why they were so competitive and jealous of Claudia and how that jealousy hindered their own self-development. It might have been a difficult exchange. One woman confronting two others with her anger about their actions is not an easy task, and yet the relationship had become untenable. The three were bound together in a destructive pattern and Claudia's anger was the signal that the situation was far from alright.

Expressing anger is one side of the issue, receiving it is another. Many women are intensely self-critical and imagine, in a difficult situation, that they are in the wrong or have not performed up to par. In hearing criticism from the outside and allowing the content of the anger to be absorbed, a woman can learn something about herself which will be far more useful to her than the fantasised guilt and self-blame she might otherwise have a propensity to feel. Freda and Melinda were close friends and neighbours in their late twenties who had been drifting apart over the last few months. Melinda was angry with Freda because she felt Freda had withdrawn from her. Freda, meanwhile, had been feeling guilty about the fact she no longer accommodated Melinda in the ways she used to. She wasn't always available when Melinda called, she didn't help her out with baby-sitting as much anymore, she wasn't a constant source of emotional replenishment for Melinda.

When Melinda told Freda of her anger, it gave Freda a chance to think about why she had been withdrawing. She realised that, for a long time, she had felt burdened by being such a 'good giver'. Melinda's anger and complaints made her aware that she had started to rebel against that role, consequently attempting friendship

124

with Melinda, and others, more on the basis of her own needs rather than theirs. But because this had been a largely unconscious shift, one she was barely aware of, she wasn't able to tell anybody about the changes she was going through. Melinda still felt angry and rejected; the explanation didn't soften the hurt. She couldn't help feeling it was something in *her* that had turned Freda off. But it wasn't, and Freda had to insist and clarify for herself that she had been a compulsive giver, almost addicted to looking out for and after others, and that her withdrawal – which aroused guilt and worry in her – was an attempt to change the basis from which she gave. She couldn't commiserate when she didn't genuinely feel like it, she couldn't any longer bury her own needs by taking care of friends' needs. She had her own experience and that had to be recognised. As we shall see in the next chapter, this recognition was expressed in the most minor of ways, but these had deep significance for Freda.

In these four chapters we have stressed the importance of women recognizing what is troubling them in their relationships with one another. We have illustrated how, in even the most minor of ways, confronting these difficulties can be exhilarating. It can encourage the relationship to grow. Much of the guilt, fear and distrust, the deep disappointments between women which lead to negative responses can be handled, when women talk to one another about their experience of each other's actions.

It is not an easy thing to do at first, but articulating difficulties, taking responsibility for resolving them, owning up to pain one may have wittingly or unwittingly caused, would be a tremendous step forward in women's relationships. It could enable the valuable and irreplaceable things that occur between women to be strengthened. It would move the relationships out of the murky area of the merged attachment into cleaner more direct lines of communication. It would enable the skills women have developed for nurturing, for empathy, for understanding – the giving which is so much a part of a woman's experience of herself – to emerge out of a sense of selfhood and a separated attachment, rather than a merged attachment.

We need to be brave and look at the difficulties that occur between women and take them on. We don't need to retreat from them, they are not insurmountable. Our nurturing skills and the genuine love we have for one another will stand us in good stead, as we take new steps in our relationships.

Reference

Over the last decade Harriet Goldhor Lerner in *The Dance of Anger* (Harper & Row, New York, 1985) and Teresa Bernadez–Bonesatti in 'Women and Anger: Conflicts with Aggression in Contemporary Women', in the *Journal of the American Medical Women's Association*, 33 (1978), pp. 215–219, have made some extremely interesting and useful contributions to an understanding of women's anger, placing women's difficulties over expressing and feeling it, within a psychosocial context.

CHAPTER 8

Speaking Up

The kinds of difficulties between women that we have been discussing are frequently exacerbated by our hestitation in talking about our feelings of envy, competition, abandonment, anger, guilt and betrayal. While many women are extremely practised at talking about how their partners, their children, their mothers, their fathers, their bosses have annoyed or hurt them, they are novices when it comes to talking *directly* with a friend about an upset between them. The mere idea of mentioning a hurt, expressing a grievance, showing a friend she has made one angry, or perhaps asking for something from a woman friend in a straightforward manner, can make her very nervous.

She may fret for hours about how to bring up a particular situation. She may talk through whatever is troubling her with another friend. She may hope that her friend will see what has transpired and repair it without her having to mention it. She may pray for her anger or negative feelings to disperse so that she doesn't have to confront her friend. So unused is a woman to discussing the negative feelings she may be experiencing towards a friend, that even trivial complaints are rarely expressed in the way they invariably are within a couple. Often this doesn't matter at all, for women can swallow the petty annoyances that are bound to occur between them. But because, in general, women are so unaccustomed to speaking up to friends about what may be troubling them, friendships that could be saved deteriorate, causing tremendous heartache and distress.

In our analysis of the root causes of the emotional difficulties between women, we hope we have provided an explanation for why, despite the proliferation of assertiveness training courses and today's emphasis on speaking one's mind, women continue to be hesitant, and barely a dent has been made in this particular area. As we have seen, a central part of what women seek in their relationships with one another is often unconscious. It is no less than the repairing of aspects of the mother–daughter relationship. Women seek support, love, and acceptance from one another. At the same time they anticipate restriction and rejection. These unconscious wishes and fears are an important part of woman-to-woman relationships. And because a merged attachment is so often entwined within women's relationships, the feelings between them can become so intense, the need for one another so strong, and the transferences so deep, that it can feel too threatening to bring up difficulties.

For all these reasons then, women rarely develop the facility of talking directly to one another about difficulties between them. Yet it is imperative that we begin to do so. If we can share with our friends more of what we feel with them – if we can accept and show that we are angry from time to time, that on occasion we are upset or disappointed, that we do feel abandoned or let down, that we suffer guilt about one another – we can have a richer exchange and better relationships. If we don't raise our difficulties with one another, we either remain stuck in a merged attachment, or the relationship becomes fractured. We develop fantasies about what is actually occurring. We can read rejection where it is not happening, abandonment where it is not occurring; we can imagine anger when it may be dormant. We watch one another, to see if we can assess what the other may be feeling, rather than articulating our own feeling or worry. In a sense, we remove a part of ourself from the relationship and take the problem into our head where it works out otherwise, without having checked first whether it could work differently in real life. We become distanced from one another or cut off from parts of ourselves. Meanwhile, the real relationship contracts and diminishes.

Speaking up is not about a moral imperative to be honest, it has rather more crucial functions. It has the potential to cut into the projections we may well be making and clears them up. Projections are a transaction in which, without realising it, one sees (projects) a part of oneself in the other. We describe another's behaviour, or translate it, based either on what we wish to be doing but can't see ourselves doing (we imagine they are angry when we are unable to express our own anger), or we load on to them responses from our past that may not be appropriate (we are angry and imagine they will cut us off if we express it). As such the relationship is a limited one. The other person becomes less a person in their own right and rather more a vehicle for one's own fantasies and thoughts.

If, however, we speak directly, express a strong feeling, or ask a friend about something which worries us within the relationship, we break into the projection. We allow ourselves to be in the relationship rather than retreating into a fantasy. And in breaking through the isolation and re-engaging in the relationship, something else is occurring too: a chink is created in the merged attachment. For, when differences or upsets can be aired, and in so far as the articulation of differences or negative feelings can be accepted, differentiation occurs. Let's take a really simple example. Two close friends, Beth and Nancy, both teachers in their forties, are discussing a third woman in the department, Georgina. Nancy really likes Georgina, she feels she is salty and cheeky, full of spunk and energy. She likes going out with her. Beth, who is also very energetic and outgoing

129

doesn't trust Georgina. She thinks she's on the make for herself and that she is manipulative. She can't bear Nancy liking her. She tries to prove to Nancy how unreliable Georgina is. Nancy doesn't try to argue about how great Georgina is, she just says, "That's not how I find her. I like her very much." Beth keeps hammering away at Nancy about how dreadful Georgina is until Nancy eventually says, "Look I'm sorry we feel differently about this, but we do and I'm afraid you'll just have to accept it. I like her and you don't."

Nancy was able to hold her own; not deny her positive feelings for Georgina, and not try to change Beth's mind either. Beth had to come to accept that they didn't always feel the same. This made her a little uneasy. She would much rather they agreed about Georgina. But at the same time, Nancy's refusal to see it her way gave her an opportunity to examine the intensity of her wish for them to be in agreement about Georgina. Beth realised that she wanted Nancy to agree with her because she felt her reality threatened if it wasn't confirmed by someone else. She distrusted her own feelings unless they seemed to be the same as her friends, and she had pushed Nancy hard on this one because she didn't like Georgina, but couldn't accept that she was justified in her dislike unless her best friend agreed. When best friends can disagree, even over a relatively simple issue such as this, there is an opportunity for the psychological basis of the relationship to shift – from one which encompasses a merged attachment, where there is guilt about differences, to one in which the two can be individuals and connect with one another from that basis.

Sally was feeling insecure. Her last child had just left home and she was at a bit of a loss. She wasn't sure now how to structure her life. Her close friend, Joan, didn't seem to have much time for her. Sally was sure it was her neediness that had pushed Joan away. When Sally finally brought up with Joan how upset and hurt she was in general, and how Joan's lack of attention had made her feel rejected, Joan was stunned. She had been so caught

130

up in her own difficulties that she hadn't a clue that Sally was upset. She felt badly about being so remiss towards her friend. She apologized for being distracted and assured Sally that it was her own family crises, and preoccupations at work, that were distracting her. It took great courage for Sally to raise this with Joan, for she was sure Joan would confirm her own fantasies. But when she didn't, when Joan said she felt sorry she had been so unavailable and that she wasn't put off by how miserable Sally was, both women felt considerably strengthened. Sally was able to cancel her fantasy about it being her upset that had pushed Joan away, and Joan felt a genuine compassion and regret that she hadn't been more available to Sally. Joan could say this without feeling guilty and without feeling pressurised by Sally. Instead of Sally accusing Joan of neglect, she spoke directly of her own pain and her own needs. Joan, in response, simply felt an obligation to be honest; not to be the all providing mother who could/could not make everything better.

The outcome of Sally speaking up, was reassuring and worthwhile. It broke Sally's feelings of isolation and brought the two women closer.

Let's look now at another simple example, but one which contains a more complex projection than that between Sally and Joan, to see how speaking up enabled a relationship – and the women in it – to grow rather than collapse.

Alison and Jill are both single and in their twenties. They became friends through working together as secretaries for the Department of Education where they have shared an office for three years. Alison is an extremely sharp dresser. She is meticulous, from manicures to matching shoes. When Jill first met Alison she marvelled at her ability to look so good every day. Jill was neat and well dressed but never thought about all the finishing touches that added so much to an outfit. In a way Jill felt it meant one was vain, if one engaged in that sort of detail. And yet she admired Alison's appearance. Several months after working together Jill began to polish her nails. She liked it and bought many different colours and manicured herself regularly. Gradually Jill found herself also buying colourful scarves, necklaces and stylish shoes. Over the three years since she had known Alison, Jill's appearance changed radically.

There was something that attracted Jill to Alison's style. It spoke to a part of Jill which was either unformed or dormant. Seeing Alison's ability to physically present herself in that way, Jill felt a kind of permission to try it herself. Alison both shaped and legitimised Jill's desire. It was within the merged attachment – that is the mirroring of Alison – that Jill was able to develop herself. In fact, eventually Jill's style differed quite markedly from Alison's, but that difference was a stage which had to evolve from the earlier mirroring one.

The difficulties began between them when Jill started to feel some hostility from Alison. Originally Jill felt Alison was supportive of Jill's new interest in her own appearance. Alison told Jill about some stores that she liked and they went shopping together in their lunch hours. At the point at which Jill was really beginning to feel good about herself, and to see that her appearance reflected some of the positive things she felt about herself, Alison seemed to distance herself. When she asked Alison questions either about work or personal matters she felt that Alison replied abruptly and coldly. Jill began to sense a feeling of competition from Alison and noticed that Alison was buying new things and not showing them to her and not inviting her to go shopping. Jill was convinced that as long as she was not a threat to Alison then Alison could be friendly, but once Jill, too, looked attractive then Alison could only be competitive with her.

It was true that Alison had become less involved with Jill and she was feeling guilty about it. Another woman who had once worked in the same office, but had been working elsewhere for the past two years, had recently returned and Alison was spending more time with her.

132

Jill's interpretation of Alison's behaviour had not taken this into account. Her fantasies about what was going on between the two of them reflected the crossroads she had approached in her self-development. Mirroring Alison had been enormously important to her. Copying Alison's clothes was, at a psychological level, merging with another woman. It represented her need for attachment and approval. Her new clothes reflected her sexuality and adult womanhood. It was a break with her mother's view of her and she could only make this break by attaching herself elsewhere (to Alison).

As long as she was getting the approval of another woman she could feel connected and therefore safe. Moving to the next stage, of diverging from Alison's taste in clothes was a manifestation of her separate identity. It was a statement of her own development and inner security. But this was a big step psychologically and she became frightened. She handled her fear by projecting disapproval and prohibitions onto Alison, inventing a scenario in which it was Alison who cut her off because of her new independence. The possibility of being her*self* and still having the permission, connection and love of another woman seemed impossible.

The conflicts that Jill experienced, which originated in her relationship with her mother, were projected onto Alison. Jill felt that she could not become an adult, sexual woman without threatening her connection to a woman she was close to. What could Jill do to try and dispel the impression she had. How might she initiate a conversation with Alison?

Jill: "Alison, I've been wondering about something. Is there something wrong, because you don't seem to want to spend much time with me?"

Alison: "Well, actually I've been aware of it too, but, well, I felt that you've been annoyed with me for some reason."

Jill: "I haven't been annoyed with you. I've missed you. You've been spending a lot more time with Mary recently. I feel you haven't wanted me around much . . .

133

why have you thought I've been angry?"

Alison: "You've acted sort of snappy and annoyed recently."

Jill: "Have I? I'm sorry. I don't know why. It's strange. I was sure you were angry with me, and you've been thinking I'm angry with you. I thought maybe you didn't like something I did or the way I behaved."

Alison: "I have felt funny about Mary coming back and I wondered whether the three of us would all get along together, and maybe I've felt I wanted to keep you both for myself."

When Jill reflected on what Alison said, she saw that she had been acting snappy and annoyed. Unconsciously she was relating to Alison as if Alison were her mother. Alison's nervousness about how to integrate her two friendships, together with Jill's irritability, were responsible for the distance between the two of them. Alison felt unsure and unentitled about having two friends, as though she were being disloyal to each, and so she cut herself off from Jill. Jill had needed to protect herself from Alison because she was trying to preserve her new 'self' and keep it away from her Mummy. By talking to Alison, Jill dispelled her fantasy that Alison disapproved of her growing self-confidence.

As soon as Jill had the courage to talk to Alison about what was happening between them, the connection was reaffirmed and actually strengthened. Alison really appreciated and admired Jill for speaking up. Although Alison had felt nervous throughout the conversation and she was left with quite a bit to think about, she was excited and happy afterwards and her interest in Jill increased.

Often broaching difficult issues, such as the coolness between Jill and Alison can bring about good results. Although it is a scary thing to do, it can reignite a relationship which is in danger of disintegrating out of misunderstanding and the unconscious projections that have occurred.

But, it could be argued, these instances of speaking

up, illustrate fairly simple difficulties. What if there is a genuine growing apart as with Christine and Andrea, strong envy as we saw with Hilary and her colleagues, feelings of abandonment and betrayal as we saw with Margot and Adeline. Surely it is pointless and too dangerous to expose these kinds of feelings? What is to be gained by doing so?

The first point to be made is that, until the tangle of issues that can come between friends is aired, it isn't possible to ascertain whether the cause is a jumble of projections, disappointments and anger due to unreasonable expectations within the friendship, or a genuine growing apart. As we become accustomed to talking with our friends about the difficulties that come between us, we can sort through these issues, and if it emerges that the relationship has become untenable, then it is possible to leave it – with sorrow and regret perhaps – but without enormous guilt or conflict. In talking about difficulties or perceptions of the other, it is obviously crucial to find a language that is sensitive and useful to both people.

It is important to find a way of talking that does not arouse guilt in the other or impose on them demands that are essentially unmeetable. There is a world of difference between telling a friend you felt let down and *accusing* her of letting you down. Telling a friend that you are angry is more constructive than exploding on her. Because women are so unaccustomed to talking directly with their women friends in this way, it is bound to be bumpy at first. We will say the wrong things, or present our grievances and upsets ackwardly. But this has to be dealt with in order that the silences and discomforts we live with can dissipate. One of the most damaging effects of the silences is that we forget how very helpful and healing our relationships with women can be. We lose sight of the capabilities our friends have to help us through our muddles. The richness we so value in our woman-to-woman friendships recedes and we have a distorted view of what it is that – when we weren't angry, disappointed, hurt – so attracted us to a particular friend. When Brenda, one of Hilary's colleagues in the Chicago Psychology Research Center, was able to tell Hilary how envious she was of the attention and exposure her work was receiving, that she didn't hate her but wanted what Hilary had for herself, Hilary and she could look at the ways in which Brenda's important research on postnatal depression could become more widely disseminated. Hilary could help Brenda see that her work was very good, that it was the capriciousness of the media that had seized on her own work on child abuse and that it wasn't, in this case, anything intrinsic in Hilary that caused her work to receive so much attention.

Hilary supported Brenda's wish to have her work better known and used. Brenda was happy to have Hilary's support and Hilary was relieved that, with Brenda, she was no longer the object of envy. Hilary didn't have to try to deny that she was getting attention or that she was enjoying it. She could have her experience and she could recognize Brenda's. If they hadn't spoken directly, Hilary would have continued to feel guilty, while Brenda would have used Hilary's public prominence as the reason why she wasn't getting more of what she wanted.

Unlike many marriages or committed sexual relationships in which arguments expose negative feelings, many friendships flounder amidst unspoken disagreements, hurts and misunderstandings. Arguments between girlfriend and boyfriend, between husband and wife are considered healthy. But as we have seen, in friendship upsets are rarely directly expressed to the person who engendered them. There is hesitation over being frank about feelings which may suggest there has been some unkindness, lack of thoughtfulness, or selfishness, on the part of a friend. Exposing emotions which suggest difference, needing to fulfil oneself (as opposed to giving to the other), or the desire for a separate experience, can be excruciating between friends. Wanting something for oneself, rather than

136

offering to share it with a friend appears selfish, abandoning; a compulsion to be tucked away rather than exposed.

Rosalie, Tessa and Donna had been very close friends in art college. After college Donna got a terrific job in a new museum that was opening in Los Angeles, while Rosalie and Tessa both stayed in their home town of New York, one to paint, the other moving into furniture design. Despite the geographic separation they continued to think of themselves as a threesome. Phone calls were frequent. Rosalie and Tessa always talked about Donna, shared their opinions about her latest lovers, how her job was going and so on. One Christmas when Donna returned to New York for a visit, Rosalie and Tessa picked her up at the airport and the three women spent the first evening and all the next day together.

The following evening Rosalie took Donna aside and 'confessed' that she wanted to spend some time during the week's visit alone with her. She said she loved the three of them being together but that she also wanted to be just the two of them. Donna agreed. At the end of the evening they discussed plans for the following day and suddenly there was an awkward silence. Rosalie looked at Donna, Donna looked at Rosalie. Rosalie said there was a photography exhibition she thought Donna would enjoy and suggested that she and Donna go and then meet up with Tessa in the afternoon. There was another awkward silence. They all agreed that would be the plan, said goodnight and went home.

On the way home Tessa felt awful. She was furious with Rosalie. How could Rosalie be so insensitive as to not invite her to the exhibition? How thoughtless, or worse than that even, how mean of her. She felt excluded, abandoned and angry.

Rosalie went home shaking. She knew that Tessa was upset and she felt it was awful to have excluded her. She didn't see how she could enjoy her time alone with Donna after this. She considered phoning them both to change the plan.

Donna returned to her parents' house feeling anxious and tense. These visits were always so mixed. She loved seeing her friends, but she seemed to get into such a mess as she tried to organise her time between them and family. It always seemed as though everyone was tugging at her and that someone would be angry with her for not giving enough. Now it had happened with Tessa. She wanted to telephone her and talk about it, but she didn't know what to say.

As long as Rosalie, Donna and Tessa were together, all was well. If they remained a group, a threesome, each felt secure in her place. Rosalie's stated desire to spend time alone with Donna challenged the merged three-way attachment. It created a division, or boundary, where before there was none. This was threatening and upsetting for each of them in different ways. Tessa's exclusion made her feel angry and competitive towards Rosalie. Rosalie felt greedy and infantile; guilty for demanding too much. Her efforts to get what she wanted left her feeling she had done something wrong. She had been unsure about whether it was alright to pursue what she wanted and so she had become sneaky. Donna felt guilty for following her own desires in the first place by choosing to live in California. She felt that on her return visits she should be available to everyone and fill all their needs. In California she was much more sure of herself, whereas in New York with friends and family, she automatically returned to her merged attachments. She hadn't been aware of her own need to be with either of her friends separately. When people's needs were confluent, she was fine, but when a divergence was expressed she felt torn, anxious and guilty. She could not choose, and she couldn't cope with the idea that someone might be left out and hurt.

While these three good friends could each imagine conversing in twosomes about the awkwardness of the situation, it was outside their experience to imagine that all three of them could talk together about the difficulty. Indeed, each of them had the impulse to call the others;

but at first it was *only to change the situation back, to make it more comfortable, to recreate the merged attachment.* Each felt so wrong in her own upset and so ashamed of her own responses that she did not feel able to share them with her dearest friend.

As it happened Rosalie did call Donna. Initially Donna thought that maybe they should include Tessa, but as they talked together, they both realised that it was ridiculous not to spend the morning together alone. When they had all lived in New York, the threesome had frequently divided into twosomes, because there were different interests between them. Rosalie felt better seeing that Donna could also assert her needs, so she wasn't forced to take all the responsibility for wanting to spend time alone with Donna, neither was she cast as the 'rejecting' person. Donna was pleased to recognise that she did have her own demands and wasn't just responding to the tug of the threesome. Then Rosalie called Tessa. At first Tessa was a bit distant on the phone, and Rosalie nearly got cold feet. She thought perhaps she should just bury the whole idea and abandon her trip with Donna. But she didn't. Since she could easily imagine how Tessa was feeling, she was able to approach the difficulty with considerable compassion. She said that this was a situation which would always crop up for the three of them when Donna was in town for a limited time. Rosalie said she could understand that Tessa might feel hurt and rejected but that she really did want to spend some time alone with Donna. Tessa listened and tried to get past her own hurt. She realised that it was a perfectly legitimate wish on Donna and Rosalie's part. She herself wouldn't mind spending an evening alone with Donna, but she hadn't even allowed herself to consider the possibility.

In this encounter, Rosalie's two initiatives – first in speaking up about her desire to be alone with Donna and then in ringing Donna and Tessa – pushed the friendship forward to a different level. In asserting herself, she gave each of them an opportunity to grow; to see that the relationship was quite strong enough to survive and accommodate different needs within it. Nobody collapsed under the weight of guilt, nobody's pain was denied, nobody's conflicts went unrecognised. The real issue with its attendant difficulties was managed.

The situation was considerably more difficult to resolve for Christine, the kindergarten teacher and Andrea, the law student, whom we met in Chapter 4. As you may recall, what each one sought in the friendship shifted, making the original basis of the friendship untenable. During their friendship Andrea changed. When she had first become friendly with Christine, she had been quite unhappy and pessimistic. She and Christine spent a lot of time commiserating with one another and agreeing about how terrible life was. But as time went on, Andrea's self confidence developed and she began to have a different outlook on life. She felt dragged down by Christine and found herself arguing with her about Christine's negativity. Christine meanwhile felt jealous of Andrea's new friend Julie, and confused by Andrea's rejection of her. What could these two friends have done that might have produced a less painful end to their friendship? Whatever was said, wouldn't the friendship have died anyway, so why make the process even more graphic and painful?

The fact is we don't know what would have happened if, instead of Andrea retreating and Christine pursuing her, the two could have talked about what was happening between them. We can't be sure that there would have been a different outcome, but there is a reasonable chance that the hurt and confusion could have lessened and, even if the relationship were not saved, its demise would have been better understood. If they had been able to talk about what was happening between them, Andrea might have said that she was feeling more hopeful and optimistic these days. Christine might have been able to say she felt rejected. If that reality were acknowledged by each of them, they might have gone on to talk about how Christine felt abandoned and how Andrea's new confidence threatened her. Andrea, in turn might have discussed how fragile her new confidence sometimes seemed, and how Christine's pessimism frightened her for she feared it might drag her backwards. This would have opened up a conversation about the dynamic within their relationship in which they had, as we saw, raged against the world together, while simultaneously denying or externalising their own pain. In other words, Andrea and Christine would have needed to address the way in which Christine continued to see herself only as a victim.

By so doing they might have been able to understand how seeing herself as a victim, trapped Christine and kept her stuck in her unhappiness and feelings of powerlessness. They might have explored how Andrea had overcome this in herself, and how and why she sometimes felt on shaky ground. If they had been able to talk with one another about Christine's unhappiness, as opposed to only raging at the injustice that was causing it 'out there', Christine could have been directly in touch with her pain. The reader may well ask why removing the defence is worthwhile; why is it better to be in pain than to feel oneself as a victim?

It is very hard to move out of a victim psychology – and the unremittingly awful feelings that surround one – unless one discovers what it shields. When that emerges, it is more likely that change can take place, and that the fantasies – of everything always being utterly hopeless until the metaphorical white knight arrives – which accompany being a victim, can be jettisoned in favour of coming to terms directly with the unhappiness. In facing her unhappiness, Christine could have developed a certain confidence. Andrea would have been able to feel compassion and empathy for her, rather than being turned off by her 'defence'.

This, of course, is the most promising of outcomes that could have occurred. It is also possible that by trying to speak with one another about what was happening between them, Christine would have raged at Andrea

141

for abandoning her and confirmed her sense of self as victim. Andrea would have felt guilty and treacherous. The relationship would have broken up with no real gain. But this outcome, while possible was not that likely, for although their friendship had included a dynamic in which their merged attachment kept out pain, they also cared very much about one another; they had been friends for a long time, they had many things in common and they had liked each other a lot. These positive aspects of their friendship may well have been able to counterbalance the upset once it had been expressed, rather than necessitating the end of the relationship.

Andrea and Christine's friendship broke down because Andrea was unable to go along with, or challenge, Christine's negative view of everything, now that she was no longer so negative in herself.

Perhaps because Adeline and Margot were social workers and accustomed to examining psychological processes, the conversation they were eventually able to have, about Margot joining a Psychoanalytic Institute for further training, could touch on the psychodynamics operating for each of them and between them. One evening shortly after Margot had been accepted into the training programme, they went out together and talked about what this meant in Margot's life, and the questions it had thrown up for Adeline. Adeline told Margot how threatened she had felt, how she had feared losing her and how she had felt the urge to apply too. Margot told Adeline how uncomfortable she had felt about telling her that she wanted to apply for the programme, as she imagined Adeline might feel critical of her in some way, or jealous.

They both felt relieved that these feelings were out in the open. There wasn't anything either could do about them, but just airing them brought them closer. They talked about the way Adeline's background had made her insecure about her choices and how Margot's departure from social work made her feel shaky. They talked about how their backgrounds prevented them feeling entitlement to further education and career advancement, and so on. Most importantly, they talked about the ways in which they were very close and committed to one another, and how they wanted their bond to survive this radical change. In the talking it became clearer to Adeline that she did not want to change her job. She was happy in social work and while Margot becoming a psychotherapist would be a real loss for her, it wasn't what she wanted for herself. Margot was able to share with Adeline how she was both scared and excited to be leaving the security of an institutional setting. Part of what made her able to do so was, in fact, the love and support she had always received from Adeline. It had helped her to feel stronger in herself and seek new avenues for work.

Because Adeline and Margot could talk, they could share their nervousness with one another. Training at the Institute was a big step for Margot and it would mean a change in their relationship. But they could see that it might also enrich their friendship, not threaten it. Through the love and support they had given one another in the past, they had helped each other grow up emotionally in significant ways. While their friendship had elements of a merged attachment (namely the panic Adeline felt which almost impelled her to apply to the Psychoanalytic Institute too), they had managed over the years to use it, if you like, to heal themselves; to find the consistent nurturing and approval they had both so needed from another woman. Having given each other so much, they were now able to differentiate and to keep a strong attachment based on their psychological separateness. They did not need to retreat back into a merged attachment.

The merged attachment that cements relationships, preventing the discussion of difficulties which occur between women, also acts as a brake on women speaking up to one another about aspects of each other's lives. Many women have discussed with us the frustration

143

they feel when they rush to concur with a friend's perception of a situation, while inside themselves they have a different view. Other women have disclosed their unease at not being challenged enough by girlfriends, even if they find they don't relish a confrontation. Such problems revolve around the issue of commiseration. Commiseration is an integral part of women's highly developed repertoire of giving. It is the capacity to show that one understands what another might be feeling, and thereby comforting her or him, often by producing instances in which one has been similarly made to feel hurt/angry/irritated/betrayed and so on. Experiencing another's support in this way can be very reassuring. The sympathy and concern, the sharing, can help one feel less isolated. But, at the same time, if the commiseration is built on an identification with the other – i.e. one actually feels what one's friend is feeling, as though in her shoes – then the sympathy isn't, in the end, of much help to the person in pain. What do we mean by this?

As we have seen, women's overpowering need for one another, and the merger and identification which is such a feature of women's friendships, brings both rich contact and immediacy to the relationship, at the same time as it may preclude or silence differences. In commiserating, one is not simply having a good moan together. There is often an implicit demand to see the situation as it is presented and, therefore, not to question the person's perceptions. Commiserating, then, can mean that one is immobilised, complying with a view that doesn't feel accurate. A typical scenario in which much sympathizing occurs, is when girlfriends discuss difficulties with their partners. Often one will say to the other, 'I know just what you mean,' and go on to detail the irritations in her own relationship. Much time may be spent together in this way, providing a kind of mutual support system. But in reality this is not that supportive for, in the confirmation, each woman may get stuck in a dreary and pessimistic view of things. The support they give one another reinforces the sense that it is 'him' who is at fault, and that there is little to be done about it except to complain together.

'He' may well be at fault, but if the woman cannot accept the way he behaves and if he is unwilling or unable to change his offending behaviour or attitude, then friends may have a greater role to play than simply to sympathize. Often it is possible to see that one's friend misperceives a situation. One might detect a pattern of responses in her sexual relationship that contribute to the difficulty. Often the friend is looking for something beyond empathy or confirmation of her own view. That view has clearly not helped alter the situation and it may be that she requires a challenge. In such circumstance the commiseration prevents an honest reappraisal.

Gwen, a booking clerk in a theatrical agency frequently moaned to Jane, one of the secretaries there, about how awful and inconsiderate her husband Paul was. Jane was sympathetic and, although she and her boyfriend had their share of difficult times, she felt generally optimistic about her own relationship. She listened to Gwen and the two of them concocted things that might induce a different response in him; but to little avail. He was inconsiderate and thoughtless and as a result he often hurt Gwen. She in turn would feel rejected and become clingy, wanting some proof of his love to counterbalance his distance and meanness. They alternated between squabbles and private wars. None of the suggestions that Jane and Gwen thought up had much impact in practice, partly because Gwen was too unsure of herself to try them out consistently, and partly because Paul wasn't open to changing. In time Jane dreaded that moment in the conversation when Gwen would detail Paul's latest outrage or the latest instance of hurt. It made her feel as helpless as Gwen. At the same time she wondered why Gwen was so stuck in the marriage. There were no children, she was self-supporting and the relationship was clearly unsatisfying.

One day when Jane and Gwen were out for coffee,

Jane found that she could not contain herself any longer and when Gwen started to moan about Paul, Jane said simply, "It's time for us to ask ourselves why you stay with him." It wasn't that different a response from the one they usually ruminated over, but it was stated in a direct manner which brought Gwen up short and made her think about it. In the ensuing conversation, Gwen revealed how she really didn't expect any better; her parents' marriage had been awful, her own relationship with her mother and father fraught. She had no expectation that things could work out well with Paul, or anyone, for that matter. It was very distressing for Gwen to face these feelings but as she and Jane talked together some of the upset about how hopeless she felt was expressed and discharged. Revealing her most intimate feelings to Jane made her feel stronger. Having them listened to and understood made her feel a little more optimistic.

Because Jane didn't reject her, or try to cover up her pain by offering false solutions to what was evidently a much deeper problem, Gwen felt some calmness. She went through a period in which she was quite depressed. Although there was no immediate improvement in her marriage, she did stop waiting for Paul to press the magic button which would make her life turn out better. The energy that had gone into keeping this unconscious fantasy alive in herself and the rage that she dispensed when he inevitably disappointed her, now became more available for other uses. Gradually she found herself reaching out to other relationships in which she did feel respected and cared for.

By adding constructive criticism on to the commiserating, Jane helped Gwen to mobilise strengths that had become dormant during the marriage. Commiseration is a skill women have developed which has both positive and negative aspects to it. Women's identifications with one another provide them with the capacity to understand, and sometimes even feel, what another is experiencing. This can bring great comfort, intimacy and

146

contact between them. But, as we have seen, this capacity often stems from the woman's search for self through identification and merger with someone else. In other words, she is able to feel what another is feeling because her own boundaries and her own feelings are so malleable. If this element is present when she is commiserating, she may be so imbued with feeling what another is feeling, sensing what another may be fearing, or knowing what the other person is repressing, that she is unable to give of herself as a separate person. Being in tune with someone else in this way, she has abdicated herself and cannot usefully contest and challenge the other person's experience. As such she is not really being as good a friend as she might be. The relationship can became static and the sympathizing an inadequate response to what is required.

Commiseration and the allied phenomenon of distorting one's own experience ever so slightly to fit in with that of a friend's, occurs so habitually between women, that even in apparently trivial exchanges, it can be very difficult to not do so. But it can be important to find a different response to a friend's upset, especially in Freda's case where, as we have seen, she was struggling hard to free herself from always seeing things from the other person's point of view. When Melinda moaned about how awful the weather was on holiday, Freda was tempted to act as she had unthinkingly in the past and to moan about something amiss on her holiday. She felt pulled into a commiseration based on a shared experience, even where there wasn't one. She wanted to say, "I know, I know, my holiday was only so-so," but that wasn't accurate, her holiday had been wonderful. She had been tempted to deny her experience to support her friend in pain, as though both of them having a bad time would make it alright. She felt dragged into giving out of the merged attachment, where everything was the same. But, as we have seen, giving out of the merged attachment in which one's individual experience is denied, actually prevents real giving. Freda would have had to

147

pretend, or tell a white lie about her holiday, in order to join with Melinda. Freda found a more satisfactory response for both her and Melinda by being genuinely sympathetic and hearing how disappointed Melinda was without having to manufacture a similar experience. Precisely because she had a good holiday she could appreciate how important it was and she was genuinely compassionate about things not working out well for Melinda. This simple example was important to Freda in many ways. It was a confirmation of her own struggle for authenticity. While from the outside it may not have seemed significant, inside Freda it was a building block in asserting herself, and not collapsing into someone else's experience.

The wish to speak up, the need to speak up and the fear of speaking up are present in so many women's relationships. But the effort is more than worthwhile. It not only clarifies difficulties in the relationship and allows the individuals to sort through the tangles and projections that exist; it almost always pushes the relationship forward to a deeper more satisfying level. The exhilaration women feel after they talk with each other about desires or upsets they felt ashamed about, is always surprising. Before the 'difficulty' is aired there is a kind of cloud over the friendship which blots out the positive parts of the relationship, creating in each of the women a kind of amnesia about why they had even liked the person in the first place. When they talk through their difficulties – and most often were not rejected as anticipated – they feel excited and strengthened both individually and in their friendships. All this can happen because this is not an encounter in 'honesty' *per se* or a mandate to 'tell it like it is'. It can happen because the compassion each woman finds in herself towards the other woman, even while hurt or angry, or the respect she can muster for herself, so that she is compelled to bring up something that disturbed her, allows her to present her case from her point of view. 'This is how I see it. Is this how you see it?' This starting point avoids encounters which, under the guise of talking straight, become attacks of one kind or another. And this perhaps is the key. To share the distress that may be engendered in a relationship the person initiating the talk has to say what *she* experiences and what *she* has been imagining to be the situation for the other person. It is not her place to say what is for the other person, to either interpret or accuse them. She should endeavour to say, 'I felt jealous,' 'I felt envious,' 'This circumstance made me angry,' rather than accusing the other of making them envious, angry or whatever. In other words, the woman needs to recognise that her friend may not have done anything to attack her, her friend's actions are more likely to be caused by her friend's own problems. She must also recognise that the feelings aroused in her, as we saw in earlier chapters, may serve as a defence against more obscure feelings. These are feelings with which woman friends can help each other. Expressing reactions from one's own vantage point help to clarify what it is that is troubling one, and opens them up to another without purposefully provoking guilt or anger. It is important that women, learning to talk with each other in this new and frank way, find a language and a form that takes account of their love and need for one another. We must trust that speaking up to our women friends will not sever the ties, it will only strengthen them.

CHAPTER 9

Friends and Lovers

The seven members of the Chicago psychologists collective we met in Chapter 5 take out their diaries to fix a date for a meeting. A variety of thoughts, reactions and feelings occur to each woman as she turns the pages. Those who are in couples share a difficult problem – how to reconcile their commitment to their women friends and colleagues with their commitment to their couple relationship. Rena has recently started living with her boyfriend and is hesitant about making arrangements in the evening, because she feels conflict about being away from him. Ann and Susanne, who each have young children, envision telling their partners about yet another evening when they will be out, leaving them to attend to the domestic responsibilities on their own. Brenda lives with her lover, Jill, who consistently feels angry about Brenda's devotion to her work, feeling that more energy and time are given to the group than to their relationship. Brenda imagines telling Jill about the meeting and anticipates the tension that will follow.

After the initial reactions each woman who is part of a couple begins to make the internal adjustments necessary to bring her*self* back into the picture. And as she connects with her own desire and genuine interest in the meeting, she feels the tugs even more acutely. She quickly makes a mental note of her partner's schedule for that week. Those with children do a mental baby-sitting juggling act, those without children suggest a night they know their partner is busy. The attachment to friends and partner seem at odds. The friendship is experienced as a pull on the couple relationship, and *vice versa*. Even for these feminist psychologists, who can lecture on women's psychology and women's difficulties regarding entitlement or autonomous desire, there is lingering guilt, a feeling of selfishness about taking so much for themselves, for overindulging, for wanting friends, partners and work. Each imagines her partner will have a negative reaction to her "other attachment," and often she is correct.

At the height of the women's movement none of these women would have predicted that they would find themselves in this dilemma. Indeed, it was one of the great breakthroughs of the early seventies that women realised how important relationships with women friends and colleagues were to them. No more, we declared, would we drop our closest female friends the moment a man called. As we encouraged each other to pursue our desires we could not conceive of the consequences this might have on the time available to spend with friends. We didn't know we were gradually shifting our priorities. We didn't know that a few years down the line, weeks could go by without our spending time with our dearest woman friend. And yet, women are, once again, it seems, placing a priority on their couple relationships and seeing less of their women friends.

How did this happen? Is it simply that we 'grew up' and moved from one phase of our lives to another? Have we, in fact, reproduced exactly what our mothers and grandmothers experienced before us? Has the transition from college or university years, with all their passion and intensity, to 'mature' adult life, followed its inevitable course? Maybe we were right all along thinking that when we reached thirty it was all over. Could it be that the intensity of our female friendships was merely a phase which is now over?

151

We think not. What has happened is not an inevitable aspect of growing older, or even an unavoidable result of having so many additional time and energy consuming commitments in our lives. Certainly these are all real constraints and difficulties to overcome but we believe that more is going on. Once again, underlying psychological forces are at work, forces that derive from what it means to be a woman in our society.

To some extent it is possible to see the reassertion of the priority of the couple relationship, as a retreat from the difficulties encountered in women's friendships. As we have indicated, the very intensity of women's relationships, the importance we have allowed them, together with the very real social changes which have occurred for women over the past decade, have in turn produced new and difficult tensions between women. In the preceding chapters we saw why it can seem easier to retreat from these emotional issues than to confront them. A by-product of what seemed like the impossibility of speaking up to our women friends about these unsettling feelings, was often a retreat back into heterosexual and couple relationships. Within the couple we could sidestep the feelings of envy, of competition, of longing, of disappointment, which we felt towards a woman friend. It was a lot easier to tell our male partner about our annoyances and irritations with a girlfriend than to tell her directly. Now, rather than telling a girlfriend about the grievances we felt towards a male partner, it is often the other way around. And we feel surprised and relieved that our men can listen to these feelings and offer support of one kind or another.

Our relationships with men, since they are obviously of a different gender, seem to offer the possibility of breaking free of merged attachments.* Male–female relationships *appear* to provide the woman with the sense

---

*Although many of the dynamics we shall address occur in both lesbian and heterosexual relationships, gender difference makes those dynamics far more obvious. For this reason we have chosen to focus on heterosexual relationships.

of differentiation and separateness that she seeks. For all its uncertainties and misunderstandings, the couple relationship is, in important psychological ways, a necessary and safe place for many women. Squabbles, fights, disagreements are more accepted in couple relationships than in friendships. Unlike a friendship, a marriage is not in jeopardy (even if it feels like it at the moment) because the partners argue. So that, although friends may disagree, feel disappointed in one another or angry, dealing with those emotions seems far more difficult. And, although women may feel enraged by their sexual partner's differences in viewpoint, the experience of being challenged, of being forced to take account of different points of view, of not having one's insights automatically concurred with, is part of the psychological attraction that men hold for women. We've seen how difficult it is for women to create this kind of boundary between each other and yet how crucial it is to do so.

This is not to paint too rosy a picture of marriage, for many women are trapped in abusive relationships, relationships in which they feel passive, or relationships in which open disagreement is not tolerated. Nor is it to suggest that women are psychologically separate within couple relationships. It is rather to explain one of the buried psychological dynamics that fuel male–female relationships, dynamics which sometimes work as an antidote to a merged attachment. For, even though couples merge psychologically every bit as easily as women do, the shape of heterosexual merger is not the same as that of female-to-female merger.[1]

The essential differences in men's and women's psychologies are important to our discussion in two ways. As we all know, male and female personalities follow in broad terms with what is considered – at any given time – appropriate for boys and for girls, for men and women. In this process towards selfhood and identity, a woman's interactions with other people provide her with a reference point. She creates and maintains a sense of self through her connections with others.

153

Women live in a network of relationships and know themselves through these relationships. Men, on the other hand, know themselves in the *difference* – i.e. in the way they distinguish themselves from others. The image of the masculine man is attractive to women because it suggests (no matter how mistakenly) the man's ability to be a full and substantial person on his own. While she cannot easily identify with this image, she may well be drawn to it as a counterpoint to a selfhood that is essentially based on affiliations.

Similarly, the defence structures of men and women – the psychological mechanisms that protect the undeveloped and hidden parts of each of us, evolve differently in childhood for boys and girls[2]. Paramount as a defence structure for men is a kind of false differentiation, a setting oneself apart from and free of others. As an infant the boy is merged with mother and in that merger incorporates aspects of her femininity. In this process of separation-individuation he utilizes her gender difference to delineate the boundaries between them. He comes to know himself through this difference. His developing masculine self is not mother. In his movement towards autonomy, he distances himself from mother and femininity and the latter becomes a buried and repressed aspect of his developing self. Later on in life, attachment and intimacy in heterosexual relationships threaten the 'false' boundaries which were constructed at a very early point in his psychological development. Thus intimacy, which threatens to touch his buried 'feminine' (undifferentiated) self, provokes a fear of the loss of the essentially masculine self he has come to 'know'.

For a woman, we've seen that a lack of boundaries, false or genuine, exists and she is easily subject to merge within her intimate relationships. Indeed, she seeks her identity through the attachment. In intimate relationships she can lose a clear sense of herself. Thus, when a man and a woman merge psychologically they both face a loss of self, but the defence structure that exists against these losses works very differently, so that *typically men crave distance while women crave closeness.* Women unconsciously look to men to provide the nurturing we associate with femininity, as well as the separateness and differentiation we associate with masculinity.

Ours may be the first generation in recent history which has begun to make significant emotional demands on men, requiring them to struggle within themselves to develop new resources for emotional contact and intimacy. Men too have changed, because of feminism and because of their own dissatisfactions with the damaging effects of being raised with a masculine identity. In many ways some women are beginning to get more, emotionally, from their relationships with men.

For women with female lovers, the conflict is posed less dramatically. Lesbian relationships benefit from the shared social experience and history between women. They benefit from the fact that two women have been raised with the capacity to nurture and to care, to initiate emotionally and to be emotionally responsive. Women lovers do not enter a different psychological mode when relating to each other, as opposed to relating to their friends. This, combined with the sexual relationship, means that the propensity to implode into a merged attachment is exaggerated. Intimacy may be problematic because the defences against a loss of self, in the merged attachment, are in ascendance. Lesbian women often feel that they maintain a sense of self in their friendships but that the sense becomes less clear within their sexual relationships. And yet, as opposed to heterosexual women, often the lines between their friends and lovers are less delineated. That is, one's lover may well be one's best friend.

For heterosexual women the division between what we want from men and what we want from women is no longer as clearcut as it used to be. Although our mothers may have longed for an emotionally responsive partner, their expectations were quite different from ours. Divorce rates in recent years have proven that unsatisfying

155

marriages are no longer tolerated to the same extent as in previous generations, where the significant attachment was made to the man, whether or not one actually got the emotional connection one sought. Women today do have greater expectations from their emotional relationships with men. The lines of attachment are blurred as the needs we have in our relationships with men and women have overlapped. We desire emotional connection and autonomy from both. And yet, as we've seen, separated attachments are a mystery to us. *Believing that we can achieve our own psychological separateness, and maintain our intimate and needed attachments to both a man (or men) and a woman (or women), are almost unattainable.*

As we've seen, both women and men alike are unaccustomed to experiencing women as separate and so assumptions are easily made, in both lesbian and heterosexual relationships, about the life of the couple taking precedence over the woman's autonomous activities. Out of her own need for attachment and her deep belief that it is she who must adapt herself to secure the relationship, the woman adjusts her life outside the couple to fit her partner's needs (or her fantasy of what the partner will accept). Unconsciously, she is busy holding onto the attachment. Her internal world is actively engaged in a juggling act both to maintain her autonomy and to not threaten the connection. She feels the potential disruption at the same time as she attempts to protect herself and her partner from the knowledge of her separateness. She acts on an unconscious knowledge of the parameters of her separateness, as she curtails and adapts her activities to fit in with her partner's.

And so we have seen a gradual realignment of sexual relationships and friendships. The marriage has become a partnership, a mutual support system which is charged with meeting more of each individual's needs. For some women this works reasonably well, for others it is a disaster. For women friends who are both in couples, the couple relationships often take over and become the *modus operandi* for social gatherings. The couples now

156

go out together to dinner or to the movies. If the women had been the original friends then they make a shift in the amount or quality of time they are now able to spend together. Perhaps they make an effort to meet occasionally on their own, but for the most part they find themselves alone together only on the telephone or when going to the ladies room on the evening out with their husbands. It may be, during those brief moments, that they manage to experience the kind of intimate exchange that once filled their lives. They have transferred their dependency on each other to their partners and, in so doing, there is a symmetry in their experience which may seem to work for all parties.

Some women in this situation know they miss the time spent with their girlfriend. They feel that something is lacking and they experience a special kind of loneliness. They are aware that relationships with their partners and children fill the better part of their non-working life and, although they may be very happy in their family situation, a part of them hungers for woman-to-woman contact. Some women make the effort to carve out time to have lunch or dinner with a friend, which they then enjoy and savour. Others may experience more tension in negotiating time with girlfriends. They may miss it, but are anxious about spending it away from their partners. They cannot comfortably and securely allocate social time outside the couple. Still others grit their teeth and go without, telling themselves that they are not alone and have no real reason to feel the sadness or emptiness they do feel. They may experience these hungry or deprived feelings as disappointment with their partner, and they begin to feel dissatisfied in their couple relationship. Alternatively, many women blame themselves for wanting too much, being too needy, and feel that the emotional yearnings are just another example of their insatiability. But for almost all women there is some degree of disappointment. Some of their emotional needs go unmet.

Where a man may be extremely helpful over discussing strategies about how to deal with a given situation, he is likely to be rather less fluent about knowing how to initiate or engage in emotional dialogues. He may become irritated by his partner's needs, feeling them as demands upon him, or he may be perplexed by her explosive anger when he fails to adequately understand something she wants from him. In the misunderstanding she feels utterly frustrated and wants him to understand her, just as she imagines a girlfriend would. It is here that we separate another strand in the intricate web of relationships. It is as though *women want women to have the capacity for differentiation that men convey and they want men to have the capacity to identify and have the emotional antennae that women have.* There is a continual search for the attachment which will provide continuity, security and love, whilst simultaneously providing the boundaries of separateness which will enable her to exist in her own right.

However much support and emotional connection a husband or male lover may provide, he cannot replace a woman friend. His experience makes it impossible for him to share and deeply understand some aspects of female experience, which a girlfriend understands effortlessly. Girlfriends are able to communicate so easily because of the wide range of their common experience and interests. A couple may go out to dinner and find that they have little to talk about. This *rarely* happens with women friends. As we've seen, women share in nuances, details and layers of multi-textured exchanges.

Moreover, a man can't replace the connectedness of a relationship with another woman, neither can he easily encourage his partner's psychological separateness. No matter how loving and caring a husband or male partner may be, he has tremendous difficulty with the autonomy and separateness of his female partner. There is a complex interaction between women's and men's emotional dependency needs[3]. Although men may appear to be less dependent and more genuinely separate, this is because their emotional dependency needs are more continually satisfied. First their mothers and then their

158

wives or girlfriends – who were raised from day one to accept nurturing and caring for others as part of their personality and their duty – provided that kind of care. Thus, by and large, emotional nurturing in heterosexual couples does not occur symmetrically. A woman comes to marriage expecting and yearning for a partner who will understand her deeply, accept her and be there for her to lean on emotionally; but all too often she finds that her partner is frightened of intimacy, steers away from emotional contact and discussion, and is somewhat frightened or put off by her needs. Whereas, in some sense, her husband continues to receive mothering, she does not. Therefore her unconscious expectations – desire for both a nourishing connection as well as a supported autonomy – are rarely achieved.

Often a woman receives sufficient nurturing from her women friends and expects very little of it from her partner. Some partners have understood and supported their lovers desire for time with women friends. They may feel some discomfort when their partners tell them they are going out with a friend on a given evening, leaving them to fend for themselves, but they make efforts to contain their unease. Their own anxiety about their wife or partner's separateness is semi-conscious. Rationally, they recognize that their partners are autonomous adults who are, indeed, separate from themselves. These men usually have been influenced by the women's movement and know that times have changed, that women no longer should be expected to be at their beck and call. To one degree or another, they are making personal efforts to examine and change the expectations and assumptions, *vis–à–vis* women, with which they were raised.

Some men encourage their partner's friendships because, it allows them time for their own work or other interests. They may feel relieved when their mates make a date with a girlfriend, leaving them to meet a friend for a drink, to do some work at home that evening, or to just relax and watch television. One of the things men often

159

find difficult about being married is the loss of the sense of freedom which they feel they have on their own. However, many men feel threatened by their partner's relationships outside the couple. A wife's attachment elsewhere signifies her separateness, and as such engenders discomfort for him. He may feel abandoned and lonely when his partner is not around and it is at these times that he feels his own emotional dependency. He may feel inadequate; if he was enough for his partner she would not need to be with others. He may act as if he approves of the friendships but make it difficult for them to spend time together.

James, a 33 year old computer consultant felt quite uncomfortable about his wife, Eileen's friendships. He saw her group of friends as strong, talkative, vivacious women. He both admired them and was scared of them. He felt excluded from their closeness, a closeness that he felt, perhaps, was missing in his friendships with other men. He felt awkward in their company and didn't know how to relate comfortably to them. He would pout when they were around or speak critically about them afterwards.

James travelled a lot on business trips and knew that during those times Eileen spent most of her free time on 'dates' with her various friends. One time when he was away Eileen had a miscarriage. James was upset for her and sad that they wouldn't be having another child right away. But when they spoke on the phone and he heard that Eileen's friend Lilian was looking after her he turned the conversation to other matters. He felt hurt that Lilian was in 'his' place. After he hung up, on thinking about it, he also felt relieved that Lilian was there because he felt that she would be able to handle the situation far better than he could. The next day when James phoned and Eileen said she was feeling a bit better he told her that, although he had completed his business, he was going to stay down for a couple of days to play golf. After all, Eileen was doing fine and her friends were doing a good job caring for her. Unconsciously, James acted out his hurt, inadequacy and imagined rejection, by rejecting Eileen. For James, Eileen's attachments outside their couple relationship were extremely difficult to tolerate. He needed her devotion and full-time attention in order to feel safe and relaxed within the relationship. Although Eileen was extremely upset by James's actions, there was a way in which she accepted it as a part of their relationship. Eileen lived with a tension between her marriage and her friendships. She was continually juggling these relationships and transporting herself back and forth between two worlds.

The primacy of the couple relationship, then, has left many women feeling, once again, emotionally hungry. We can now see more clearly a current dilemma for women in couples. On the one hand as they find themselves more enclosed within the couple, there is a part of them which is aware of feeling isolated and, at times, alienated from the person to whom they are now closest. On the other hand the pressures of work and children, the desire (conscious or unconscious) to avoid the new conflicts and discomforts with women friends, the psychological construct which has us giving up our attachment to a woman, in order to attempt separation, leaves women with an intangible emptiness; an emptiness which, we would suggest, derives from a lack of sufficient time and contact with other women. It is an emptiness which is a painful reminder of some critical aspects of the mother–daughter relationship.

As girls we were unable to receive both the continuity of connection, love, and acceptance from mother, as well as the boundaries of differentiation and psychological separateness. We 'left' that relationship, burying the pain of what we didn't get. In our relationships with women we recreate that merged attachment, hoping to regain the connection and make up for its loss. Yet we have so much difficulty achieving the second part of what was needed – boundaries and separated attachments. In childhood we learned that we must transfer these needs for connection from mother to a man; now

161

we replay that very same scenario. Just as we remember the taste of the satisfying, containing, fulfilling aspects of our attachment to mother, so too do we now remember the bonds with our women friends. What we really need, and perhaps what women find most impossible, is to have *both* satisfying couple relationships and meaningful attachments to women friends.

Ruth and Norma began their friendship when they were both in their late twenties and both single. They spent nearly every weekend together and shared the ins and outs of their various and ever changing love affairs with men. Ruth was the first to marry and at that time Norma was seriously involved with Joe. The couples went out together and Ruth and Norma continued to spend time on their own. Norma and Joe began to live together and for the following two years the friendship continued on a smooth course. Then Ruth and her husband, Adam, split up. During the time of the separation and divorce Norma was very involved and supportive. Ruth was a mess. She spent many evenings with Norma and Joe, even sleeping at their flat on the nights that she felt too upset to be on her own. She was worried that she was an imposition but both Norma and Joe kept assuring her that she wasn't. Gradually she began to recover from the divorce and to feel her old self again. She fixed up her apartment, replacing things that Adam had taken to his new place. She still found it difficult and unusual to be on her own, but the acute pain was now a thing of the past.

Ruth and Norma still arranged regular dates with one another, but now their availability to the friendship was no longer parallel. When they were both in couples their need for each other matched perfectly. Now Ruth felt a gap between them. This was particularly acute at the weekend when Norma was spending time with Joe. Ruth felt very much on her own. She knew that she could not expect Norma to go out with her on Friday or Saturday evening because this was traditional couple time, but it was precisely at those times that she felt most

162

acutely alone and in need of her friend. She felt very awkward going out to dinner or to a movie on her own and had to push herself each and every time. She found herself waiting for Norma to suggest a date, because she didn't want always to be the one who seemed interested or needy. Because Ruth was not in a couple her dependency on Norma was more apparent. Although she knew that Norma was dependent upon her as well, Norma's dependency was somehow hidden within her couple relationship. Ruth was already feeling too vulnerable and exposing her need, even to her best friend, made her feel humiliated. At times it felt as though the whole world was in couples, her best friend was happy and loved, and that she would never again live a 'normal' life.

Meanwhile Norma, too, had to adjust to the change in their lives. She recognized that Ruth's situation was a very difficult one. She knew other women who were single or divorced and in their thirties, who felt desperate about the possibility of ever meeting a suitable man. Norma was aware of Ruth's need for a friend who could be much more available and she felt inadequate about providing that kind of companionship. She loved Ruth and her own need for Ruth didn't diminish. She often felt guilty for having Joe to go home to and imagined the pain and loneliness that her best friend must be experiencing. At times Norma felt she was pulling herself in two directions. Neither Joe nor Ruth actually did anything to contribute to that feeling. In fact, each seemed very sensitive to and aware of her attachment to the other. In therapy Norma discussed the way in which she was always apologizing to one or the other. She suffered from a continual feeling that she was either neglecting Joe or Ruth. She found herself fighting with Joe more frequently, feeling that the relationship had deteriorated and that she might have to end it. She was also increasingly annoyed with Ruth. One minute she didn't like Ruth's passiveness, the next she didn't like Ruth's demands. As these responses were explored in

163

therapy we came to see that Norma was having difficulty in maintaining two close attachments, one with a woman and one with a man. Her anger with each of them was a distancing mechanism. She was not comfortable with that much love and security. She felt undeserving of this luxury. She felt guilty in relation to Ruth, knowing she had something that Ruth wanted but didn't have. It seemed so emotionally unfamiliar to her having each of them accept her attachment to the other. *Her attachment with one signified her separateness from the other. Thus her multiple attachments caused her anxiety.* The 'pulls' she experienced were of an internal nature and were, in fact, pulls at her merged attachments. Her guilt and anger towards each of them represented her internal juggling act – distancing herself first from one and then the other in an effort to preserve the equilibrium of the merged attachments.

This difficulty in believing one can have a loving attachment to both a man and a woman at the same time has historical roots. We've seen how women transfer the original merged attachment with mother to their relationships with other women as well as into their relationships with men. And, just as psychological separation and autonomy presented difficulties within the mother–daughter relationship, so too do we anticipate those very same restrictions within our couple relationships and friendships. In other words, as we experience our husbands or lovers as mother, we unconsciously feel the pull not to abandon them. Attachment elsewhere, which represents a step towards separateness, seems to threaten the original relationship.

Another dynamic which may be occurring simultaneously is that for many women, whose mother's marriages were obviously disappointing, having a fulfilling and satisfying relationship themselves can feel like a betrayal of mother. It exposes what she did not have; it exposes her loneliness; it exposes her pain. Our unconscious loyalty to mother finds us sabotaging potentially good relationships, for how can we 'leave' her all alone?

We must stay with her in the sadness, the deprivation, the emptiness. It is very difficult to have so much, when mother had so little.

For many women having both a loving relationship with a man and loving relationships with women friends presents a variety of problems. Having both can feel like having *too* much. It is difficult to feel that deserving, that entitled, to so much love and security. Because (unconsciously) we did not feel that we could have mother and then move on from that relationship into the world of other attachments, having one attachment brings with it the fear of losing the other. In addition, because traditionally so few fathers share in the nurturing and raising of children, it is rare for us to have had a secure and loving attachment to both mother and father. Thus, having the love of a woman friend and the love of a male partner is unfamiliar territory.

Ruth and Norma were each grappling, from different positions, with these complex dynamics. A whole new dimension was added when Norma became pregnant. She felt extremely anxious about telling Ruth. She knew Ruth would be happy for her, but how could Ruth help but feel awful at the same time? She told Ruth about it over a lunch date and Ruth responded with genuine excitement and pleasure asking appropriate questions about the due date, antenatal care, etc. Neither woman presented what this might mean to their relationship, although they were each privately wondering. When they parted Norma felt relieved the news was out and appreciative of her friend's ability to be so emotionally generous. Ruth, on the other hand, was flooded with thoughts and feelings. She was truly happy for Norma and Joe. She loved them dearly and knew the pregnancy was making them very happy. She felt frightened about the impending changes in Norma's life, knowing that once a baby was born Norma would be even less available to their friendship. She felt a deep sadness that she and Norma could not share this experience together, just as they had done with other milestones in their lives. She felt frightened at the thought that she might never have a relationship in which she, too, could have a baby.

Over the months of the pregnancy things changed only slightly. Norma talked with Ruth about the pregnancy, the birth plans, and her ideas for part-time employment. Ruth continued to talk with Norma about her work, her occasional dates and her despair about the dating scene. They were in two completely different places in their lives, but their friendship was such that it could weather those differences. Then the baby was born. Ruth knew that things would be different, but the extent of Norma's involvement with the baby went far beyond her expectation. In the first months of Tessa's life Norma and Joe seemed totally absorbed. Every conversation, every interest, was related to Tessa. Ruth loved Tessa and felt closer to her than she ever had to any baby, so to some extent endless discussions about every aspect of Tessa's development were of interest. But Ruth found herself having to make another significant adjustment in her relationship with Norma. Norma's attachment to Joe and now to an even more dependent Tessa meant her availability to the friendship had decreased dramatically. Going out on their own became a rare treat. Ruth knew, rationally, that this was nothing to do with Norma losing affection for her, for she could see that Norma had very little time to herself, but it was painful and difficult nonetheless.

As several months went by Norma began to feel like her old self again. She longed for some time with Ruth and other women friends alone and yet she found it very difficult to find. She already felt guilty for going back to work and being parted from Tessa for so many hours, and so arranging social dates for herself was terribly fraught with tension. She tried to chat on the telephone with Ruth several times a week and felt that Ruth was very understanding about her circumstances. They both seemed to hold onto a knowledge that as Tessa got older things would ease up and they would have more time together.

Norma and Ruth's situation is currently being reproduced in the lives of thousands of women. These two women were able to maintain their friendship through three significant life changes: marriages, a divorce and the birth of a child. Other women have not been as fortunate. In recent years we have heard of many friendships which have not survived these kinds of changes. At times the differences have created too great a gap, making identification, a central feature in women's friendships, impossible. Some women have found they could not handle the feelings of envy or competition which emerged as a result of a friend being in a couple, having a baby, or perhaps divorcing and getting out of an unsatisfactory relationship. To witness a friend having or doing what one would like for oneself can make continuing contact too painful. But surely the loss of a woman friend, the loss of that special and much needed woman to woman contact, is just as painful.

Perhaps now, precisely because women are struggling to create and maintain their separate identities, it is for the first time possible for women to have attachment both to friends and lovers. Attachment that does not stem from a merged attachment, but rather from a genuine, separated attachment. The stresses and strains of managing work, partners, children and friends are very real. At times it feels as though there aren't enough days in the week to manage them all. But women are experimenting, adjusting, and juggling their time, in order to have the things that feel necessary for a sense of well-being. Maybe women today cannot spend as much time as they once did, or as they would like, with their women friends. But in breaking free of our merged attachments, and, more importantly, by forging new *separated* attachments, we can hope to make up for the loss of quantity with a new quality of women's friendships; friendships just as rich, just as intimate, just as caring, but also more flexible, more open to difficulties and differences. We cannot afford to sacrifice the ones we need the most. In developing a new feminine identity, a separated identity, we must believe in our entitlement to the love of others, both women and men, so that the meaning of separateness will include attachment.

References

1. Eichenbaum, Luise and Orbach, Susie, *What Do Women Want?* (Michael Joseph, London, 1983).
2. Stoller, Robert J. *Sex and Gender: On the Development of Masculinity and Femininity* (New York, 1968).
Eichenbaum, Luise and Orbach, Susie, *What Do Women Want?* (Michael Joseph, London, 1983).
3. *ibid.*

CHAPTER 10

Separated Attachments/ Connected Autonomy

Eight women psychotherapists, between the ages of thirty-four and fifty-eight, meet in London to discuss their work and break down some of the isolation that comes with private practice. Two of the women have grown up children, four have young children, two women do not have children, though one is planning to get pregnant in the coming year. Into the third session the group is talking about stress. Stress related to work, to juggling work with raising young children, to earning enough to pay for the flat which must now be bought. Stress related to insufficient time for relaxation or fun. Stress related to not having enough leisure hours to spend with husbands and partners. Stress related to the pressure to read technical material, to continue to learn, when one can barely find time to pay the bills. Sighs of acknowledgement are heard throughout the room as a woman speaks. Giggles of recognition punctuate the sentences. The personal experience of losing a baby sitter is heard one moment, while the next they speak of capitalism and the ways in which feminism has been corrupted, taken over, dragging us along with it. The personal and the political all in one discussion. There is something thrillingly reminiscent of earlier times.

169

As the women talk about the stress in their lives there is both the pain of the reality, as well as a feeling of hope and optimism. Once again, here we are, women talking about things that do not feel right, being critical of the system that directs us to these points, questioning our choices, our options. Women together sharing the new wave of isolation they feel; guilt about not being with our children or partners enough; envy of the success of other women; anxieties that arise when making the decision about whether to read a journal article or relax and read a novel. There is relief in the sharing. Joy as the other women nod their heads in understanding and agreement, when what we feared was disgust and rejection. The stress that we were speaking about seemed to dissolve bit by bit. Women supporting women. Women being accepted and cared for by other women. Personal pain and self-hatred being translated into social critique.

There was also something noticeably different from a women's group of fifteen years ago. Each woman was professionally defined. Each woman earned an adequate income. Each woman either had children already or had come to some resolution about getting pregnant, or not having children. We were no longer talking about the constraints of women's traditional position. We were no longer facing the enormous hurdles of establishing ourselves in the world outside of the home. On the contrary, some of the women expressed longing at the mere thought of spending uninterrupted time with their children or pottering around the house. Things have changed.

Although this is a particular group of women reflecting a particular profession, class and ethnic make-up, the issues they spoke of, in many ways, represent the concerns of a multitude of women today. For, whether or not one was an active agent in changing the social position of women, one cannot escape the impact of these changes. And, as with other significant social movements and reforms (civil rights for example), at one

170

moment the results seem to have been incorporated so gradually as to be nearly unnoticeable, while at another viewing, one sees that truly dramatic social changes have occurred in an historical blink of the eye. We live in a new era. The era of women working outside the home as well as in the family; the era of rising divorce rates; the era of an increase in single women and women without children; the era of childcare; the era of shifting domestic and economic responsibilities.

The women in this new women's group were fortunate enough to be able to sit down together to talk about their concerns. By admitting to the feelings which each previously held inside herself, out came the hope, the optimism, the energy, which to some extent counteracted the isolation, the depression, the self-hatred, the guilt, the anger. Another noticeable and monumental difference in this 1980s women's group was the number of times a woman said, "Yes, I know what you mean, but I don't experience it in the same way. For me . . ." One was able to listen to another's feelings and predicament, to feel empathy, to offer support and yet not have to be either the same as or keep quiet about the differences, in order to preserve the feelings of safety. For the most part each of the women could tolerate and acknowledge that there were eight individual women in the room. Yet could still feel the support and the care from another woman. This most important occurrence reflects the historical progression in womens' psychology. For, in this new conscious-raising group was the ability of the women to be separate, individuated people who were also empathetic, caregiving, loving and connected. *The differentiation did not dissolve the connection. The psychological achievement this represents and the significance of this social and psychological development feature, is a key to the resolution of the current crisis in women's relationships.*

Throughout the pages of this book we have observed women who are struggling with the critical issues of separateness and connection, in relationships with other women. Over and over again we have seen how one

171

seems to threaten the other, how difficult it is for a woman to feel she can get support and love from another woman, without offering her very self in exchange. We have seen the ways in which our psychologies, developed and shaped in very particular ways within our culture, have us colluding in the repression of our-*selves*.

And yet, within every form of oppression lies the seeds of liberation. While women have suffered because of our history, in which the division of work has been based on sex, this division of labour has nevertheless produced specific sensibilities in women. The responsibility of raising infants and children demands attention, care, concern and awareness for the well-being of another. The mother–child relationship sensitizes women to the needs of others. As the managers of the domestic, personal and emotional spheres, women have retained an ability for human connection. Our traditional, restricted social roles are as enablers, because they develop our ability to connect and nurture: but they are also disabling, because they restrain our autonomy and separateness. In the same dialectical fashion, the patriarchal context of the world women are now emerging into – the 'masculine' world of competition and repression of emotions – has its liberating aspects, because these features encourage, even demand self-development. This will ultimately produce a new synthesis, a new femininity that is connected and caring, as well as separate and defined.

In the 1980s we are witnessing the tension between a traditional mode, which seeks to incorporate some women into it, and far reaching change which reveals the need for more social and psychological equality between women and men, in the world inside and outside the home. The traditional way aims to put the brakes on the gains of the 1960s for women and blacks, and by taking in a token number of each, declares we have been successful and need demand no more. But what has really changed, if one accepts that vision? Is it that we are now allowed the honour of being more like men? Do we want that?

We think not. Men, too, have suffered as a result of this competitive, alienated form of social relations. Men have been severely emotionally constrained and disabled by the mandates by which they have had to live. Far from needing women to be more like men, we need men to be more like women. That is, not only do women need to have more freedom to develop their creative potential outside of the domestic sphere, but men need to develop themselves *within* the domestic sphere. In Chapter 2 we discussed some of the effects of women entering the 'male' milieu. And, throughout this book, we've seen the damaging psychological effects which have resulted from the social restrictions women and men have suffered. The social and the psychological go hand in hand. Changes in one produce a ripple effect in the other. In many ways we have all moved along on the wave of history. We've made choices, but those choices are themselves produced by the social climate of the time. What seems like an appropriate choice at one point may be just that, and yet further down the road we reflect and see that perhaps the choice has led us on a path we don't want to be on. And so we make another choice and keep moving. More and more women and men seem to be coming to an awareness that following the traditional path for men is not the road to personal satisfaction. Stress, high blood pressure, heart attacks at an early age, drinking problems, alienation from one's children and partner, need not be reproduced. Striving for autonomy, for psychological well-being and separateness, whilst maintaining a balance of connectedness in our relationships with partners, friends, and children, seems to be a route which, more appropriately, promises to meet the needs of women, men and children.

Creating the balance between autonomy and connectedness is becoming ever more critical, both socially and psychologically. It has been our intention to show that it is within women's friendships that the historical conflict of these two forces is apparent. The feelings of competition, envy, abandonment and betrayal are symptoms of this conflict. We've seen that within each of these feelings there is an expression of the wanting, the longing, the desire for self-actualization, and the rage at restrictions and oppression. The current expression of these feelings is personal and isolating and pushes each woman who feels them into further retreat. These feelings divide women and distance them from one another, leaving them to feel mistrust and fear.

It is now, perhaps more than ever, that the social and psychological pieces overlap in such a way that women need something quite specific from each other. We have shown the ways in which the 1970s reproduced, in many ways, aspects of the earliest years in the mother–daughter relationship. That is, the acknowledgement of the need for other women, and the respect and love each woman received as she gave it to others, sowed the seeds for further self-development. And yet, just at the point where we had perhaps attained a taste of self-love, the first step towards separation-individuation, we stopped short. Firstly, the forces and power of patriarchy reached out to us and allowed some of us under its wing. And secondly, we stumbled over the process of differentiation and separation. Having never had the experience of successful and permissible separation and differentiation, we could not adequately provide it for one another.

Today women have the possibility of allowing each other differences; of supporting the choice to become mothers or not; of recognizing the differences in the lives of single women and women in couples. We have the opportunity to acknowledge our need for other women as well as our need for recognition and acceptance of our autonomous selves. This time around we can offer this to each other.

Two women, separate yet connected. Each woman feels whole within herself. Each woman feels her continuing need for intimate relationships with both a woman (women) and a man (men). Each woman is able

174

to see the other for what she is, as distinct and differentiated. Each woman feels seen in this way by her friend. Each woman feels secure in her attachment to her friend. Each woman acknowledges the interdependency between them. It is within this kind of woman-to-woman relationship that giving is possible. A giving, not based on need and identification. A giving, not based on a need to connect in order to exist. A giving, not based on a search for oneself in the attachment. A giving, not based on a merged attachment. But, rather, a giving which draws on women's ability to listen, to empathize, to feel, to extend a hand, to care, while remaining separate.

Some women fear that if they were able to care for themselves, if they were alright, if they no longer operated out of merged attachments, then they would not need anyone. They would no longer want to give to anyone else. They would be alone. In fact this is never the case. For the more internal security one has, the easier it becomes to be more vulnerable and more emotionally open. One's expression of need becomes an acceptable aspect of emotional life, rather than a dreaded exposure of an insecure or inevitably lacking self. With a clear boundary between self and other, the more one has the resources for both giving and receiving.

Moving from merged attachments to separated attachments is an enormous task, and yet we are half way there. We know that our feelings are not just about separation and autonomy, but they are also expressive of the desire for connection, for nurturing, for intimacy. And, as we have seen, for all the women we have described, the ability or the desire to connect with other women is present. The familiarity, the identifications, the tools of emotional responsiveness and caregiving resonate for every woman, in her relationships with other women. Women provide other women with feelings of safety, excitement, calm, warmth, intellectual stimulation, *joie de vivre*. Whether it be women friends sitting in the park watching their children together, starting a business together, shopping together, sharing

175

a lunch break together, or collaborating on a book together, the *camaraderie* and connection fulfill a basic human need. In striving for separated attachments we are not at square one. We have a strong foundation upon which to build. For women do know how to connect, do know how to give care and attention, do know how to be aware of the needs of others. We must believe in those connections enough, trust them enough, rely on them enough, acknowledge them enough, to let go of the merged attachment. Only, this time around, we will let go from a position of plenty, of love for ourselves and, therefore, other women, of knowing we can still have more, of knowing that letting go is a giving birth.

Book List

Brief booklist on women's psychology, friendship and object relations

Belotti, E.G., *Little Girls* Writers & Readers, London 1977

Block, J.D. & Greenberg, D. *Women & Friendship* Franklin Watts, New York 1985

Chodorow, N. *The Reproduction of Mothering. Psychoanalysis and the Sociology of gender.* University of California Press, Berkeley 1978

Dinnerstein, D. *The Rocking of the Cradle & The ruling of the World* Souvenir Press, London 1978

Eichenbaum, L. & Orbach, S. *Understanding Women: A feminist Psychoanalytic Approach* Penguin, 1983

Eichenbaum, L. & Orbach, S. *What Do Women Want?*, Michael Joseph, London 1983

Faderman, Lilian, *Surpassing the Love of Men*, The Women's Press, London 1985

Fairbairn, W.R.D. *Psychoanalytic Studies of the Personality* Routledge, Kegan Paul, London 1952

Friday, N. *Jealousy* Collins, London 1985

Guntrip, H. Schizoid *Phenomena & Object Relations Theory*, New York 1969

Klein, M. *Envy & Gratitude* Hogarth Press, London 1975

Lerner, H. *The Dance of Anger*, Harper & Row, New York 1985

Mahler, M., Pine F., & Bergman A., *The Psychological Birth of the Human Infant*, Hutchinson, London 1975

Margolies, E. *The Best of Friends, The Worst of Enemies*, The Dial Press, New York 1975

Money, J. Erhardt A., *Man and Woman, Boy and Girl: The Differentiation and Dimorphism of Gender Identity from Conception to Maturity*, John Hopkins Press, Baltimore, Md 1973

Orbach, S. *Hunger Strike: The Anorectic's Struggle as a metaphor for our age*, Faber & Faber, London, 1986

Rubin L. *Just Friends: The Role of Friendship in Our Lives* Harper & Row, New York, 1985

Spitz, R. *The First Year of Life: A Pyschoanalytic Study of Normal & Deviant Development of Object Relations*, International Universities Press, New York 1965

Raymond, J. *A Passion for Friends*, The Women's Press, London 1986

Rich, A. *On Lies, Secrets, and Silence*, W.W. Norton, New York 1979

Winnicott D.W., *The Maturational Processes and the Facilitating Environment*, The Hogarth Press, London 1965

Winnicott D.W., *Primary Maternal Preoccupation; Collected Papers*, The Hogarth Press, London 1958